IF IT WEREN'T FOR THE CUSTOMER, SELLING WOULD BE EASY!

Product Knowledge + People Knowledge = Sales Success

Dr. Lewis E. Losoncy

DC PRESS
A Division of the Diogenes Consortium
SANFORD • FLORIDA

DC Press works with companies and organizations of all sizes to provide bulk quantities of this and other titles at discounts.

Published by DC Press
2445 River Tree Circle
Sanford, FL 32771
http://www.focusonethics.com
407-688-1156

This book was set in Trump Medieaval
Cover Design and Composition by Jonathan Pennell

Library of Congress Catalog Number: 2006921703
Losoncy, Lewis E.
If It Weren't For The Customer, Selling Would Be Easy
ISBN: 1-932021-18-3 [10-Digit]
ISBN: 978-1-932021-18-9 [13-Digit]

First DC Press Edition
10 9 8 7 6 5 4 3 2 1
Printed in the United States of America

DEDICATIONS

To

Every Sales Professional
Who Considers a Satisfied Customer
a Type of Paycheck.

To

The worldwide community of Salon Professionals, and Matrix Distributor Sales, and Store Professionals. You thought you were selling shampoo, and you found that you were making the world a more beautiful place.

ACKNOWLEDGMENTS

THANKS TO MY EDITOR and creative genius Gabrielle Losoncy. Despite your responsibilities with Voices and your other challenges, you found time to contribute to the book. Special thanks to Dennis McClellan, simply the most competent publisher I ever met. You do what you say you will do. And to Dennis' son, Mark McClellan who has the ability to electronically erase the crises a writer faces.

And thanks to the professionals who are growing Matrix, especially our leaders Francesca Raminella, David Craggs, Ketan Patel, and Cynthia Pitchford, who are taking the Matrix Dream around the world. Special thanks to the Matrix field staff of educators, sales professionals, marketing, and support staff.

And finally, to Diane and Gabbie for being there — *selling* me on the belief that I could meet the deadline.

ABOUT THE AUTHOR

Lew Losoncy is one of the world's leading experts on encouragement. Known as "The Doctor of Encouragement," he is a psychologist and author of 17 books on the topics of encouragement, motivation, teamwork and positive attitude. Dr. Losoncy is corporate psychologist for Matrix Essentials, a division of L'Oreal, North America's largest producer of professional beauty products.

Other recent books by Losoncy include ***Turning People On***; ***Today: Grab it!***; ***What Is, Is!*** with Diane Losoncy; ***The Motivating Team Leader*** with Don Dinkmeyer; ***The Skills of Encouragement*** and ***The Best Team Skills***.

"Dr. Lew" has spoken in all 50 United States, most of the Provinces of Canada, throughout Australia and New Zealand, as well as Mexico, France, and England. He has appeared on *CNN* and *CBS This Morning* and in media as varied as *The Wall Street Journal, Psychology Today*, and *Talk*.

He lives in Wyomissing Pennsylvania, with his wife Diane and his daughter Gabrielle.

PUBLISHER'S COMMENT

WELCOME TO ONE of the most unique books you'll ever find on the much-over-published subject of *"sales"* and *"selling."* During the 35 years I've spent in sales, you can only imagine how many books I've purchased...how many I've read (or attempted to read)...and how many I've actually kept in my library. You might also venture a guess on the number that truly had an impact on my approach to selling. Answer: few!

What you'll find between the pages in this book isn't ivory tower. It isn't pompous and full of itself. There are no inflated stories or examples that fail to relate to the real world in which you live and work. Here are actual, practical, down-to-earth, easy-to-implement tips and suggestions that are based real approaches that have worked and continue to prove themselves effective.

Implementing just one of these a week will make you a more skilled and valuable salesperson. Since there are 100 tips and suggestions, you've got a real treat ahead.

Implementing just one of these a week will make you a more skilled and valuable salesperson. Since there are 100 tips and suggestions, you've got a real treat ahead.

In my own case, over the years, I've been a very fortunate person (not lucky...fortunate). I got a great education by attending some of the finest schools in the United States. A boyhood dream to become an archaeologist and actually dig at a major historical site was realized. And I got to teach my favorite subjects to eager and willing high school students (unfortunately, many educators can't make that statement). Then, when I least expected it, a door opened, and I had to make the most important decision of my adult life.

A sales rep for a major U.S. publisher — a man I had met on numerous occasions — offered me an opportunity to interview for his sales position and territory (since he was being promoted to management). I had been in the military during the Vietnam War and had faced other challenging experiences throughout my life, but this was the most intense decision I had faced. With a young child and dreams for the future of my growing family facing me, deciding to enter sales wasn't easy.

When I began to look back, sales wasn't all that new in my life. I just hadn't thought about it. As a young boy I delivered a weekly newspaper and had to collect cash for the subscriptions. I had sold bottles of vanilla throughout my neighborhood to raise money for band uniforms. In my teens I took a job selling hamburgers and pizza at a swim club. And during my early years in college, I had worked at Gimbels Department Store in Philadelphia selling bathrobes. But it finally hit me that I had held down a major sales position when I worked as a high school teacher. Selling ideas and concepts to kids is one of the most important sales roles in the world. If you can get students to buy what you're selling and enjoy the process, you're a success.

If I took the sales position and entered the world of professional sales, I wanted to be proud of my role and make an outstanding living at the same time. I took a deep breath and went to the interview, addressed all the questions I was asked, had all of my questions answered, and walked out telling the interviewer that I was ready to make the commitment. I was in seventh heaven, hoping and praying that the numbers he had thrown at me were real and not a fabricated and imaginary puff of hot air. With out a doubt, this was the best occupational decision I had made in my life to that point.

Selling is — and should be — a proud and honorable position. When taken with pride and determination, selling can afford people a means to reaching any and all of their dreams. In my case, I took on my sales position - selling textbooks to schools and later, selling legal books to attorneys and physicians — with an understanding that I was providing a unique product that professionals couldn't exist without. My customers believed in the products, they believed that the products I sold them actually made them better at their jobs, and they believed in me. I believed in what I was selling and my customers/clients believed in me. As Dr. Losoncy says, *"Selling is Believing."* And that's the truth.

How very grateful I am that someone had spotted me and gave serious consideration to interviewing me — eventually offering me an opportunity to join one of the greatest professions available to men and women anywhere in the world.

Have you ever noticed that the one thing that always (and I mean *"always"*) holds up a sale is the customer? This fact never changes. Without the customer standing in the way, sales could be completed a lot faster and with greater ease. No joke. If we didn't have customers standing between us and the completion of the order, we certainly could move a lot more product and move it faster. Nevertheless, without customers, it wouldn't be called sales — would it?! We need customers to make it a true sale. And customers need us in order to be sold. Without this combination, sales just don't exist.

Selling isn't always easy. As my father once said (and as ***your*** father or mother most likely said as well), *"Anything worth a good income is also worth hard work. If it comes too easy, you most likely won't respect it or how you achieved it."* For a person who never sold for a living, my father was right on.

While selling isn't automatically easy, there isn't any reason why it should automatically be difficult either. That isn't meant to be a conflicted statement. Not at all. A great product, product knowledge, planning, and self-confidence are just some of the components that combine to make for successful selling. Customer resistance and rejection are also part of the dance we call selling. Successful salespeople understand and expect to face these put offs. *"Easy selling"* is a phrase often applied to a sales success — that is, after you have done your homework, showed up on time for the appointment, brought the proper support or documentation in anticipation of customer opposition, and kept your calm and addressed all objections and challenges...and then closed the sale. Afterward the word "easy" can be used with confidence. Why not? It's going to keep you pumped when getting ready for the next selling dance.

Over the years I have been exposed to some of the most humorous and often-nerve-wracking selling situations. You most likely have your own horror stories. In my case, after all has been said and done, I believe they all added together to make me the successful salesman that I became — and remain.

Years ago, I walked into an attorney's office in Charlottesville, VA. It was late on a Friday afternoon in July (you know...as the clock was ticking toward the official start of the weekend). It was your standard *"cold call."* Since it was at the southern tip of my sales territory, I had traveled over 200 miles from my home in Baltimore and had brought my wife and two young boys with me. They were back at a hotel swimming their hearts out while I walked the streets, sweating and looking for that elusive end-of-the-week sale. However, nothing was going to stop me from making this last call of the day (even though the little devil on my shoulder was whining and begging me to call it off).

The sound of my shoes entering the foyer of this pre-Civil War house (now turned into a lawyer's office) echoed throughout the building. From down the hall a voice called out, *"Do I smell a salesman?"* How right could he have been? *"Yes, sir,"* I replied. *"You have a good nose."*

Through another doorway entered a man dressed in a Matlock-style seersucker suit. With a strong handshake he offered me a *"Coke-Cola"* and followed his hospitality with the statement, *"I'm not buying anything today."*

We sat in his spacious office, a window fan blowing air across the hot room. I began the dance (hopefully taking the lead) — similar to the way a wild turkey tries to attract the attention of one of the females in his flock. *"Tell me what you practice. What type of law is most important to you these days? Are there any cases pending that could use a boost?"*

His response was eye opening and educational. *"I specialize in accident investigation with a special interest in airplane accidents."* Could this guy have written the script any better? My publishing company carried the most respected treatises on accident investigation, reconstruction, and litigation. I couldn't believe the opening he had just handed me. Not only had he given me an ice-cold *Coke* (a *"Coke-Cola"* as it is often called in the South), but an opening for me to do my dance!

I kept calm, asked questions, and let him speak — actually letting him be the star. I countered with comments about books that we published and how they would give him the edge he was looking for in an important case he had just acquired. After what seemed like a rather short amount of time (only because it was all going so smoothly), he turned to me and said, *"Do you remember that I said that today I wasn't buying books? Well, I might have spoken prematurely."*

With that said, he turned to me and asked what would it cost to pick up the books I had just described to him — and wondered out loud about any possible discount if he wrote a check. I kept my cool, did my calculations, and came back with a figure that put a lump in my throat. I heard myself say, *"That would come to just a tad over $10,000.00 and there would be no charge for shipping."* $10,000! What a great end-of-the day and end-of the week sale.

He didn't hesitate and told me to *"Write up the order. I've got a picnic to get to. I'm already late."* I wrote up the order, got his signature, took his check, and walked out of that Charlottesville attorney's office with an entirely new look at the week — and the wonderful weekend to come. Sales had become the greatest profession that God had ever created. And I believed in my heart that I had made the best choice ever when I accepted that offer years earlier.

You most likely have your own tales. The longer you sell, the more stories you'll accumulate. Some will be heroic epics where you were the white knight who helped a customer slay their dragon. Others will be full of pathos and cause you to remember what went wrong and how you'll "never let that happen again." And still others will be a litany of customers who became more than customers because you provided them with tools, products and/or services that proved you were a competent salesperson — and someone they could trust and rely upon. Those feelings can't be beat.

As for me, selling continues to be part of my life. Today I run my own publishing company. I'm still in sales, no matter how you cut it. It's just a different form of selling.

I've worked with companies of all sizes in the sale of bulk quantities of my publications to them to be used for all manner of purposes. Sometimes I come across a company that wants to do some form of internal training. Every so often I come across a company that has a product they want to promote and one of my books might just serve them well in making their customers happy while making their company look like heroes. What a great event when that happens.

As described by the author later in this book, I once walked into a situation that called for what I refer to as "*tap dancing*." You know what I mean. You enter a potential sales situation, the customer tells you what they want and what they expect...and then they throw you a curve, opening a door that you had better recognize and close quickly in your favor. In this instance, I was told in advance that if I did my job, I might just walk away with an order of 500 to 2,000 copies of a book. The meeting started with the potential customer telling me what they wanted and what they expected. My job, as they put it, was to make the numbers work — in other words, give them the price they wanted. If I did, the sale was mine. If I didn't, I could take a hike.

During the discussion, which was largely lop-sided (in their favor), I was told that a new product was about to be introduced and our book could possibly help the company in promoting this product at a specific level of distribution. However, as I listened (and that is surely a key to successful selling), I heard the door opening. The creaking sound was deafening. I heard another level of distribution actually being mentioned — a level that might increase the number of books they could use. And, if this increased number were possible, I'd have to have a number (a cost) in mind when I finally stopped "*listening*" and started "*talking*."

When I finally heard enough, took a small but deep breath, and opened my mouth, the tables turned. They turned in my favor. I suggested another level of distribution that they hadn't considered and threw out numbers that I had been calculating in my head (and on paper) while they were doing all the talking. When the dust had cleared, I wrote up (and they signed) an order for 16,000 copies of the book. And the order went from one small, anticipated amount, to a figure over eight times higher.

What a thrill for everyone involved: them and me. And what a feeling of success that gave me. This was a feeling that more than twelve years later, still makes me smile.

I don't have any outstanding tidbits of wisdom for you. My experience has shown me that if you have a true desire to succeed, you will allow your native abilities to combine with the experience and success of others you meet to produce your own unique sales approach. It doesn't take a doctoral degree to understand that some of your abilities might need honing and that some of the experiences others will share with you aren't really right for you to emulate. But with sincere planning, study, and execution, combined with good advice and leadership, coupled with advice gleaned from publications like this one, you can become the sales leader that you want to be. The choice is really yours.

Dennis McClellan, *Publisher*
DC Press

We'd like to hear from any of you and would appreciate it if you would share your own horror stories, your fun stories, and your success stories. DC Press will collect your correspondence and periodically put stories up on our website and possibly in a future reprinting or updated edition of this book.

If you do submit your stories, you can do so by contacting ***info@focusonethics.com.*** *Place your story into an e-mail message (directly in the text or as an attachment). All stories must be signed and have an accompanying physical address (street, city, zip), contact phone number (including area code), and e-mail address. By submitting your story to DC Press, you are giving permission for your story to be reprinted either in book or Internet format. Because authenticity is important, your name will be used.*

Thanks for your consideration.

INTRODUCTION

THE FORMULA FOR SALES SUCCESS

Product Knowledge + People Knowledge
= Sales Success

EVERYONE SELLS, EVERYDAY. BUT YOU ARE A SALES PROFESSIONAL!

THE STARVING ARTIST isn't starving because he can't paint; it's because he can't sell! Selling is the expertise that moves the world. Selling is such an everyday experience in life that everyone is constantly selling.

- As a psychotherapist, I was paid to sell my patients on a new attitude.
- The minister, priest and rabbi are selling their members.
- My attorney neighbor is selling his client, the jurors, the other attorney, and the judge.
- Hospitals are selling their services to the public. "Get your operation here!"
- Doctors are selling their patients on a new lifestyle.
- The audiologist is selling hearing aids.

- Listen to the President's next message, and you'll hear selling.
- The best teachers are selling their subjects to their students.
- Lovers are people who represent selling at its best — there is a lot at stake.
- And your children were selling within a few months of life, using tears, tantrums, smiles and hugs.
- Do you know anyone who isn't selling?
- And when you hear someone argue, *"I'm not a salesperson, I'm no good at selling,"* allow the person to go on and on, while you listen attentively. When the person stops talking, respond enthusiastically, *"You sold me!"*

While most people are constantly selling indirectly, you are fortunate. Your work is more direct, clean and up front. You chose selling for a living!

SELLING CHANGES THE WORLD

Think about it. As a sales professional you encourage your customers to explore better products and services to improve their lives. You could say that you change the world in a small way with every sale. Think about the hundreds or thousands of people who have directly or indirectly benefited from your products. And think about how many would not have received those benefits without your encouragement.

Plus, in the process of improving peoples' lives, you are growing personally and professionally constantly refining your own interpersonal and motivation skills.

In addition to benefiting your customers and growing socially and intellectually, you are earning a good to a great living.

Not bad, is it? Not many professions offer all of these benefits?

FROM THE DYNAMIC IDEAS OF SALES PSYCHOLOGY, YOU WILL LEARN:

- How to help your customer take a chance and get that better quality product
- How to encourage in a social context with more than one buyer
- What words to use that are absolute or hot
- How to avoid the nasty *"Boomerang Effect"*
- How to use the *"Sleeper Effect"*
- How to deal with *"Post Purchase Cognitive Dissonance"*
- How to earn instant rapport and trust
- When to employ logical rather than emotional approaches
- When do you use the *"Foot-in-the-Door Technique?"*
- When is the *"Door-in-the-Face Approach"* more effective?
- How to become an expert in the field of Sales Psychology

FRINGE BENEFITS OF MASTERING ENCOURAGEMENT

By learning encouragement, everyone around you, from your family to your friends will benefit from your encouragement. Selling is not only encouraging for your customer, client, patient or pupil. You'll find that selling is going to be encouraging for you.

THE FORMULA FOR SALES SUCCESS

Product Knowledge + People Knowledge = Sales Success

Over the past 25 years, I have been studying some of the great sales professionals, in settings ranging from the road to the business, store or shop. My goal was to discover, from a psychologist's vantage point, if there were common characteristics, such as certain human relations skills, strategies or techniques that these million dollar sellers employed. I coupled this eye-opening, and sale-closing information on these great sales professionals (the sellers) with knowledge about the customer's personality, needs and buying styles (the buyers). These insights are based on research related to selling success from the fields of consumer motivation, social psychology, personality theory, merchandising, marketing, persuasion, influencing, and the art of encouraging people. There were five major questions that the observations and research attempted to answer.

1 What people skills do the best sales pros have that make them successful?

These are the people skills that my research revealed were common amongst the leaders:

- empathic understanding of the customer
- believability
- enthusiasm
- caring
- warmth
- respect
- persistence
- optimism
- positive focusing
- accessibility (communicating that they will be there if needed)

When you think about it, aren't these the same qualities that any encouraging person has?

2 What personality needs do customers have that affect their buying choices?

Customer's have (1) product needs, and (2) personality needs. I focused on understanding a customer's personality needs that affect her buying choices. Here are a few:

- achievement needs
- consistency needs
- dominance needs
- exhibition needs

- financial motivation needs
- individuation needs
- security needs
- status needs
- stimulation needs

These are the same ways an encouraging person understands peoples' needs.

3 Why do people resist buying a product they need?

The best sales specialists recognize ten resistance styles to buying:

- the active resistor
- the passive resistor
- the conscious resistor
- the non-conscious resistor
- the personal resistor
- the change resistor
- the anxious resistor
- the loyalty to your competitor resistor
- the cost resistor
- the quality resistors.

Each resistor is discouraging him or herself from buying your product. What does he need? An encourager!

4 What specific buying styles do people have that influence their decisions?

There are many customer styles that influence the effectiveness of a sales presentation. These include (1) sensory representational, and (2) attitude styles.

Here are a three customer sensory representation styles:

- visual customers
- auditory customers
- kinesthetic customers

Here are three attitude styles:

- thinkers
- feelers
- doers

Encouragement involves understanding customer's sensory representational and attitude style and selling their customer based upon their personality, as well as their product needs. This is true customer satisfaction, isn't it?

5 How do the million dollar sales professionals keep themselves going?

From a sales psychologist's vantage point, the best of the best sales professionals are self-motivated. How do these self-starters keep themselves going?

- they are driven from within, not needing to be pushed from outside forces
- they are being self-determined

- they build on their strengths, rather than dwelling on their deficiencies
- they focus on their goals, not on their egos
- they turn rejections into learning experiences
- they feel strong personal pride in success
- they experience thrills in observing customer satisfaction
- they maintain optimism even against all odds
- they discard ineffective approaches, rather than blaming the customer
- they grow from criticism

WHY DOES EVERYONE WHO SELLS NEED THIS BOOK?

Product Knowledge + People Knowledge = Sales Success

THIS BOOK PROVIDES you with a hundred strategies and over five hundred practical tips to master the people knowledge part of the sales success equation. While selling involves selling products, these products are sold to people. And, in the end, these people, consumers, customers, clients or patients, make the final decision to buy or not. Your success is determined by your knowledge of your customer's needs; that is knowledge of both their (1) product needs, and (2) personality needs.

The average sales consultant spends uncountable hours learning product knowledge. Product knowledge is crucial because you must know the features and benefits of the products you are selling. This is the "*what*" of selling. Unfortunately, product knowledge is only half of the formula for sales success. The other half of the secret to selling success is people knowledge, or the "how to sell who" factor in selling.

The most neglected aspect of a sales person's training is in the second area, people knowledge. People knowledge, or the human factor in selling, involves developing knowledge about people, their personalities, their needs and their decision-making styles in buying. For example, imagine that you are selling two customers, with two different personalities, one with security needs, the other with novelty or exhibition needs. Each of these customers looking at the same product, even listening to your similar words, might have a dramatically different reaction.

A salesman who has an understanding of people knowledge simply brings that knowledge of each customer's needs in the presentation? The new car, stereo or hairstyle is sold differently to the security seeker than it is to the novelty seeker. And, in the end, each customer finds both (1) her product and (2) her personality needs fulfilled. Now that is complete customer service, isn't it?

Or suppose that your next customer is moved by emotional sales appeals, while the following one buys from logical appeals. Offering the same product knowledge pitch to both almost guarantees you are going to lose one of the them! That's a given. This book offers insights for you to assess each customer's buying style the minute you meet the person. These clues to determine whether you emphasize an emotional or logical appeal are subtly revealed in the customer's dress and demeanor, including her handshake, mannerisms, even the expressiveness in her face, eyes, and arms.

This book also addresses how to recognize, understand, and encourage an auditory person one minute, followed by a visual customer the next, and then a thinker, followed by a feeler, than a doer. The impulsive and the compulsive individuals both need your product, but each needs your product to fulfill a different personality need.

As you know, selling is about people. You learned that from the truest labs of life out there in the streets, the School of Hard Knocks, sales training programs, a motivating sales manager, and caring seasoned pros sitting next to you at long sales meetings. This practical hands-on knowledge is sometimes equivalent to university level courses in psychology and interpersonal relations skills. I know; I taught both. In fact, a sales person's typical comments to the ideas in this book are, *"Wow, I understand this stuff. I never realized I knew so much about psychology."*

Questions such as, *"How do I deal with the passive resistor, the cost resister or the change resister or even the loyalty to my competitor resistor?"* are discussed in these 100 ideas of selling with encouragement.

ENCOURAGEMENT SELLING IS ETHICAL SELLING

The encouraging sales professional is guided by two clear ethical principles.

First, never lie about the products. The doctor, the psychotherapist, the teacher, minister, priest and rabbi would view lying as wrong and unethical, and the same standard holds for selling. Plus, the value of a product to a customer is only as good as the salesperson's words. Sometimes that means the salesperson has to lose a sale because the product cannot do what the customer needs done.

The second ethical principle that the encouraging sales professional lives by is to always present the product in its best light. It is the responsibility, as an employee to an employer, to know and show the potential of the product to the customer. Both of these ethical principles usually go without even saying to the seasoned sales professional.

THE MOST EFFECTIVE SALES PROFESSIONALS ARE ENCOURAGERS

The best of the best of the sales professionals do more than sell products. These sales leaders use both product knowledge and people knowledge. They are encouragers. They build relationships. They understand their customer's needs. They vary their presentation from customer to customer based upon the psychological cues they read in the words and body language of their customers. In fact, they don't have a "*pitch*," but do as much listening as talking.

> *I made notes on what I saw them do, say, and think. I observed how they related to their customers. How they dealt with objections and resistances, even how they encouraged people to pay up on their bills. These conclusions, coupled with practical insights from psychology related fields, led to these one*

hundred ideas and strategies to encourage, influence, persuade and sell. No point takes more than a few minutes to read. Each approach is immediately applicable. The ideas are listed in alphabetical order so that you may easily re-locate any strategy that you found meaningful. You may pick up any idea on any page, in any order.

CONTENTS

Product Knowledge + People Knowledge = Sales Success
The Most Effective Sales Consultants are Encouragers

10 BUYER RESISTOR STYLES

100 ENCOURAGING SALES IDEAS

NOTE: Check each idea you use, as well as make a note about what you learned. Add your own examples and teaching these encouraging concept to others will reinforce them in your own mind.

10 BUYER RESISTOR STYLES

There are many motives why a person doesn't buy. One may be that the product isn't right for this person. The encourager is sensitive to this and builds a relationship with the customer anyway. The customer may return in the future or share with others the great experience she had with this sales person. Some of the most dramatic stories in this book were the result of a persistent sales person who built the relationship in the absence of a sale, in one case, for years! When the sales encourager concludes that the product does fit the person's needs and the person still doesn't buy, than the encourager analyzes why, by determining the customer's resistance style.

10 CUSTOMER RESISTOR STYLES

1. The Active Resistor
2. The Passive Resistor
3. The Conscious Resistor
4. The Non-Conscious Resistor
5. The Personal Resistor
6. The Change Resistor
7. The Anxious Resistor
8. The Loyalty to Your Competitor Resistor
9. The Cost Resistor
10. The Quality Resistor

1 THE ACTIVE RESISTOR

"I don't want your product because of reasons A&B."

The active resistor is up front with you and reveals the specific resistances for not buying. You know exactly where the active resistor stands. If you can overcome reasons A&B, the active resistor will buy.

As you know, selling is challenging. Active resistors are welcomed sights because the selling task is less complex and less confusing. Simply overcome the active resistor's objections. In this book you will learn strategies to encourage the active resistor. Once you learn the specific objections, ask the active resistor, "So if we can overcome A&B, you would be interested, right?" There is the sale. Listen for the specific objection, overcome the objection, and the sale is made.

But, and I don't need to tell you, selling situations are often more complicated than that, because resistances exist on many levels. That's why we need to learn psychology. What happens when you do overcome the customer's objections, and the person still doesn't buy? Well, you know how frequently the customer uses active resistance as a shield for other reasons for not buying. His style is not truly as simple as active resistance. But why is he still not buying after you overcome his objection?

2 THE PASSIVE RESISTOR

"Your product looks interesting, but I'll have to think about it. I'll call you."

We have a problem here, don't we? You and I know that call will rarely come. Yet you are convinced your product is right for this person. The passive resistor often acts like she is very interested "uh-huhing" you during your presentation. The passive resistor will often give you time, but will still take those cell phone calls and interruptions, but with grace, of course. There are a lot of smiles and a lot of "buts." This person isn't quite buying, but is always leaving hope that she might walk out with your product. And to add even more frustration, the passive resistor gives you no specific resistances that you can grab hold of to overcome. You just hear global thoughts like, "looks interesting," and "I see." Unlike dealing with the active resistor where you know the objections you have to overcome, the passive resistor just smiles, and leaves you only with the hope of a future phone call.

Your key is to get the passive resistor to talk. You will learn strategies of listening, empathy, warmth, respect, asset focusing and questioning throughout this book that will help you create encouraging conditions for your customer to be honest.

3 THE CONSCIOUS RESISTOR

"I need a product that will do this and this and it needs to be in this price range. Your product can't do what I need."

The conscious resistor is aware of the reasons why he is resisting the product. Note that the conscious resistor may be active or passive. If he is also an active resistor- he is right out in front with you with why he doesn't want your product. When the conscious resistors are passive, he is aware of his resistance, but isn't saying. The key to recognizing the conscious resistor is that you know that this person is fully aware of the reason why he isn't buying, and if he is conscious active, he will tell you the reason why.

To analyze whether your customer is a conscious or a non-conscious resistor, sense whether he is aware or not aware of the reason he is not buying. If his resistances are conscious, your task is to fill the bill he orders. You will learn strategies such as desired product qualities and associated states strategies to encourage the conscious resistor.

4 THE NON-CONSCIOUS RESISTOR

"Uh, it sounds good, the price is OK, but there is just something that doesn't feel right. And I can't get a handle on it."

The non-conscious resistor isn't exactly sure of why he doesn't feel comfortable with your product. He is unaware himself, that is, his resistance is not even conscious to him. Even though this person would like and could benefit from your product, there are subconscious and unconscious reasons why he isn't buying. For example, as you find in this book, some people, with low self-esteem, feel guilty about looking too good, because they aren't worth it. Or they don't deserve the more elegant car or house, even when they could very easily afford them. The non-conscious resistor is discouraged and needs your encouragement to bring out their courage.

You will learn approaches in this book to communicate your respect and belief in your customer, and to speak in more absolute words to reassure and offer appropriate guarantees whenever possible with the unconscious resistor.

To better understand the non-conscious resistor, recall times in your life when you wanted to buy something, but there was something holding you back that you couldn't quite understand. These non-conscious resistances could be something as complex as the color of the product reminded you of something that triggered a bad experience in your past. The selling relationship becomes crucial in helping the non-conscious resistor to feel comfortable to explore his genuine thoughts, feelings and reactions to your products.

5 THE PERSONAL RESISTOR

"I wouldn't buy a thing from YOU!"

You know how much the personal resistor needs your product, may even by dying to get your product, but doesn't like you personally. This is tough for the freshman salesman. "I didn't even do anything to get him mad at me," the salesman tells his sales manager. The veteran sales manager knows that these moments, as Willy Loman says in the play, Death of the Salesman, go with the territory." While the ego driven sales person has a tough time turning this customer over to another sales pro, the goal driven salesman wants the business to make the sale, and suggests a new salesman for the customer. Either way, the personal resistor ruffles the salesperson's feathers, and ego.

Curiously, chances are the problem isn't you—but rather the personal resistor, may be displacing the anger he feels towards sales people in general or even his wife, on to you. Or maybe you he is competing intellectually with you, and wants to create a power struggle. Perhaps he is projecting his own distrusting nature on to you. As you learn more about the psychology of selling, you will stop taking the personal resistor personally.

6 THE CHANGE RESISTOR

"Well, its just that I have been using this product for five years and, well, if something isn't broke, why fix it?"

How often have you heard, "We always did it this way?" This is a sure tip off that you are in the presence of a change resistor. The change resistor doesn't buy simply because she doesn't want any change and is closed to any new ideas. The change resistor will often avoid even giving you a chance to present your product because she knows if she likes it, than she is faced with the painful decision to make a change. And change is stressful to her.

The encouraging sales professional is not discouraged by the change resistor who doesn't want to listen to her presentation. "It'll only take a few minutes. New information never hurts, does it?" the sales professional offers. The change resistor protects herself up front from change by avoiding exposure to it. Yet, you know that this product has so many benefits over her current product. Encouragement selling is extremely effective with the change resistor.

You will also find practical strategies to encourage your customer to get excited about change invoking memories of some of the most exciting moments of her life. These were moments of change. And she remembers people who resisted change when she grew up and she knows that she is not like them.

7 THE ANXIOUS RESISTOR

"Well it looks good and all that, but there are a lot of loose ends, and I just don't know. I don't think I better take a chance on something I know so little about."

Anxiety = uncertainty. Anxiety, as you will be reading, is the tension we feel when we are experiencing uncertainty. The anxious resistor resists your product because he is confused or uncertain about some aspect of the product or the situation. This person may be clouded by the terminology, the product, how it is used, the terms of the agreement, or even your own accessibility after the sale. No resistor style needs the encouraging sales professional more than the anxious resistor. Encouragement can help a person develop the courage to explore the uncertainty and to take the "un" out of uncertainty.

You will discover though you use of reflective listening, you can get closer to the anxious source. And then offering reference groups, testimonials, personal stories, proof and removing the uncertainties, you can encourage your discouraged customer who wants this product to have the courage to go for it.

8 THE LOYALTY TO YOUR COMPETITOR RESISTOR

"Well, you see, I like your product, but I have been buying from Joe for years and he's always treated me well."

"My brother-in-law sells life insurance." "I buy from my neighbor." "I've been getting my supplies from Joe at your competitors for over 25 years." These are tough, aren't they? The loyalty to your competitor resistor is objecting because of a tension he experiences in how he will tell your competitor and his friend that he is no longer buying from them. As an encouraging sales professional what keeps you going is your awareness that your product can benefit him. Even though he needs your product, he is limiting or even hurting himself because of previous decisions. This person is often a pleaser and wants the approval from others. This person's resistance may be operating at either a conscious or non-conscious level.

You will experience approaches to help the customer loyal to your competitor to realize that his buying decision, with his money, should be based on his needs. He is the customer, after all, isn't he? (You will also discover that this last sentence uses a tag line). How do you unfreeze a commitment that the loyalty to your competitor resistor has made in the past?

9 THE COST RESISTOR

"Its just too expensive. I can get something similar for less somewhere else."

The cost resistor focuses in on one thing, the bottom line. Or, you can reframe that to mean, "I'm interested in getting as much value as you can for your dollar, right" (tag line). "I understand your feelings here." (Empathy). "Why pay more than you have to? Makes sense to me." (Logical appeals)

When you respond in such a way you'll notice your customer is nodding his head up and down. You will find that he have gotten your resisting customer into an agreement mode. Through the use or mirroring and matching strategies discussed in the book, as well as the similarity attraction principle, you will be able to communicate your understanding of the importance of cost. And you can proceed with the realization that your customer is thinking, "I will give you a fair shot and buy your product if you can show me that your product has just as much value for the dollar as any I can get.

10 THE QUALITY RESISTOR

"I think that your competitor's product performs much better than your product."

The quality resistor resists buying anything that isn't of the best quality. The quality resistor considers quality more important than money. The quality resistor may even be offended with too much of a discussion on money because you, the sales person should no that money is no object for a person like him!

As you get intensively immersed in this book, you may notice that the quality resistor has needs for superiority and status that he earns through his having the best of everything. Wouldn't that insight find you approaching this person dramatically differently than the other resistors?

MATCH THE CUSTOMER WORDS AND BELIEFS WITH THE APPROPRIATE RESISTOR STYLE

(Answers upside down, bottom of this page)

1. "I know what I need. I need a product that will do this and this, and it needs to be in this price range. Your product doesn't do this."
2. "Frankly, I wouldn't buy anything from you."
3. "It's just too expensive. I'm a bottom line guy and I won't pay a cent more than twenty dollars."
4. "Well, I really like your product, but I've been buying from a different company and have been dealing with the same salesman for years."
5. "Uh, it sounds good, but there is just something that doesn't feel right. I just can't quite get a handle on it."
6. "I don't want your product because of reason A & B."
7. "I'm looking for a product that will work. I don't care what it costs, I want the best."
8. "If something isn't broke, why fix it?"
9. "Well it looks good, but there is too much uncertainty."
10. "I'll have to think about it. I'll call you."

A. The Active Resistor
B. The Passive Resistor
C. The Conscious Resistor
D. The Non-Conscious Resistor
E. The Personal Resistor
F. The Change Resistor
G. The Anxious Resistor
H. The Loyalty to Your Competitor Resistor
I. The Cost Resistor
J. The Quality Resistor

A. (A) 6, (B) 10, (C) 1, (D) 5, (E) 2, (F) 8, (G) 9, (H) 4 (I) 3, (J) 7

ROLE PLAYING TO UNDERSTAND RESISTOR STYLES

Involve another sales person and each read the 10 resistor styles. Then role-play, one of you being a sales person, the other a customer with one of the 10 resistor styles. Ask questions and see how long it takes for the sales person to diagnose the correct style. And as you read the book, role play again and use the ideas from the book to encourage that specific resistor style. Role playing is not child's play — it is a serious training tool.

LET'S BEGIN!

You are about to learn 100 ideas to advance your life as a professional sales person and encourager. Take many notes and try every idea over the next year. To get even better, put your own examples in for each idea and teach this course to others.

1 ABSOLUTE WORDS

When true, use reassuring words, "always, "never," "ultimate," and "best."

Could you picture the hair stylist Arnold Schwarzenegger selling a coloring service to his client by telling her, *"maybe you'll like it?"* More likely, Mr. Arnold would look directly at his customer, smile and strongly reassure, *"I have a color that is perfect for your look. You are going to love it."*

Despite standing behind the strength of his badge, Deputy Barney Feif of Mayberry RFD wasn't convincing the 6 year olds not to cast their poles in the "No Fishing" hole, with his tentative "uh's" and, "maybes."

Arnold uses absolute words; Barney is tentative.

Absolute words communicate that the encourager has complete confidence in this product, as well as in the customer's need for this product. For example, *"After listening carefully to you, I definitely recommend this product for you."* In this sentence, **definitely** is the absolute word. Doesn't sound like there is much doubt in the sales person's mind about this, does it? Sounds more like Arnold than Barney, doesn't it? Absolute words offer the customer a solid sense of certainty, thus reassuring the customer. Especially the anxious resistor.

- Some other absolute words include *always, never, completely, guaranteed, certain, perfect, ultimate and supreme.*
- List some other absolute words you can use with specific products you sell.
- Proceed with certainty as you talk up your product.
- Assume the sale, absolutely. Your positive belief adds value to your product.
- Feel the customer gaining reassurance through your words and demeanor.
- Where might you make use of these absolute words in your sales presentation?

ACCESSIBILITY

2

"Subtly communicate you will be there for your customer, whenever he needs you."

I don't know how he does it. He's the busiest man in Tulsa, Oklahoma as general manager of a prosperous distributorship, but Kelly Heuther almost always answer his phone personally. And then Kelly gives you as much time as you need until the problem is solved. A person's accessibility is communicating to others that *"I am available, approachable and safe."* Accessibility is the subtle positioning of the encourager to the customer that *"I will be here for you. I am accessible."* There are many ways of communicating your accessibility.

"I've been with our company for 11 years."

"I'm only a phone call away."

"I live down the street."

"So then our children probably go to the same school."

Accessibility creates a sense of security in the customer's mind. *"This is not a fly-by-nighter, and if I have a complaint, I have someone I can call."* The bigger the purchase, the more important that accessibility is communicated. Remember, accessibility is most effective when it is done subtly, not obviously. One very good Canadian sales consultant communicated to his customer, *"I'll see you at exactly 10 o'clock on Tuesday,"* thereby reinforcing his solid accessibility.

- Who are some salespersons you know who are or were effective at communicating accessibility? What are or were some subtle strategies they used?
- Communicate where you can be reached if necessary.
- Be able to be counted on.
- Return phone calls as soon as possible.
- Volunteer to help out, carry the product out of the store for the customer.
- Never say, *"I didn't get back to you because I was busy."* Everyone can read through that. The best that is communicated is *"Everything else was more important than you!"*
- How do you communicate your accessibility to your customers?
- Where can you apply accessibility?

3 ACHIEVEMENT NEEDS (CUSTOMER)

- What are some other clues of a customer being motivated by achievement needs?
- Which of your products fits best with a person who has an achievement motivation need?
- Have instructional manuals available and in sight of your customer.
- Talk to your customer about previous tasks he mastered.
- If you also are achievement motivated, let yourself go without competing.
- If you are not achievement motivated, keep that to yourself.
- Communicate your respect for the achievement motivated customer.
- Think of your customers who are moved by achievement needs and how you can fulfill those achievement needs with your product.
- How could you make use of selling achievement needs through your products?

"Show your customer with achievement needs how your product can help her reach higher accomplishments"

Her face is smudged. She's Home Depot's dream girl, but she'd never ask for help. He's taken on the challenge of teaching himself the Chinese language. Or the neighbor insists on putting the complex grill together. Who are these people? They are your customers who are motivated by achievement needs. And they love challenges!

A customer motivated by achievement needs has a strong desire to accomplish things, to master difficult tasks, to be the best at something, to solve problems and puzzles, and they go after the five star difficulty level of Sudoku! An encourager observes achievement motivation when the customer talks about overcoming obstacles, winning competitions, displays trophies, or reveals personal accomplishments.

The encourager makes a note of the achievement needs, and, if possible, couples the product being sold with these achievement and mastery needs of the customer (See coupling). *"My product is a bit harder to learn to use, but once you master this, you'll be one of those rare few who has the best,"* is an example of selling a product to fulfill the achievement needs of the customer.

Notice that understanding your customer's achievement interest is not manipulation, but your heightened desire to fulfill his personality needs through your product. And, of course, be sensitive to the fact that a customer who doesn't have achievement needs may experience your comments as involving too much work.

ADAPTING HIGHER PRINCIPLE

4

"Upgrade your customer, and you create a new baseline. Once you color his gray hair, you will color his hair forever!"

There's a lot better way to fly! The US Airways agent in Paris surprised me with an offer, *"We'd like to put your family up front in Envoy Class into Philadelphia today?"*

"How much would that be?" I asked.

"Its on USAIR since you are a good customer."

The experience was so tremendous, our daughter Gabrielle begs to go Envoy Class on USAIR whenever we fly. Not any other airline will be quite the same. The agent adapted us higher, and made a loyal customer an even better customer!

Doesn't it happen to you constantly? Think of every area of your life, and how, at some point, you upgraded higher from clothes, shoes, TV, stereo, car, house, restaurants where you eat, on and on.

The adapting higher principle is the customer's tendency to continually adapt to new levels of needs. What was once acceptable is no longer acceptable as the customer takes what yesterday appeared to be a luxury, today becomes the new standard. Who would go back to watching any television from their past again? Doesn't each car a person purchases tend to be an upgrade over the previous one? CD systems are a must in cars today, going way beyond just radios. And satellite radios or even a global positioning system in a car, once viewed as a luxury to a customer, through adapting higher, become a necessity. It would be traumatic if you couldn't locate the closest Greek restaurant by a simple push of the button in your car, wouldn't it? Through adaptations, wants become needs.

Since it is much more difficult for a customer to downgrade or to, "adapt lower," the encourager continually creates new, higher levels to fulfill the customer's needs to feel herself growing and improving growing and improving needs.

- Upgrading may be in size, in quality or in quantity.
- Develop a logical sequence of upgrades of your products for your customers.
- Lowest level:
- Second level:
- Highest level:
- When a person shows interest in a certain level, give the person a taste as well, of the next higher level.

5 AFFILIATION NEEDS (CUSTOMER)

"Sell your customer with affiliation needs the social, and membership benefits of your product"

Everyone has a friend like Frank Macey. He opens up his wallet looking for a card, and there are 75 membership cards for every club, association, affiliate, and grocery store in town. He is past president of one, and headed for a meeting to another, all the while raising funds for a third. And he knows everyone, everywhere you go. He is linked, connected and is "in the loop." Frank is your ultimate source of leads. After selling him your product, give him awesome service, include him a as special member of your club or focus group, use him as an advisor, referral source or testimonial, and the new customers will come calling. He is the customer who loves connections with people.

A customer with affiliation needs likes people and enjoys being with them. Customers with affiliation motivation needs have many friends, join organizations, clubs, love new trends, and "are with it." Affiliation needs are belonging needs. The encourager senses affiliation needs when the customer reveals many membership cards, talks about attending all these meetings or is involved in many causes. The encourager couples the product being sold with the fulfillment of affiliation needs.

Think of a customer who exhibited affiliation needs. How did you recognize those needs? How can you use affiliation needs selling in your work?

- People with affiliation needs are encouraged by people who recognize their ability to connect with others.
- *"How's Mr. Popularity, today!"*
- *"Is there a club in which you aren't a member?"*
- *"You are one of the greatest net workers I've ever seen."*
- "Get leads from the person with affiliation needs."
- The person with affiliation needs is thrilled to offer testimonials to his friends about your product.
- When you reach the platinum level in purchases you earn the right to become a member of our education club."
- *"Our fitness center,* (our development) (our restaurant) (our salon) (our bookstore) *is really a community."*

AGREEMENT MODE

6

"Never use the word "but," again when disagreeing with your customer! Replace "but" with "and," and stay in the agreement mode"

Ultimate rapport is evidenced when the salesperson and the customer are in the agreement rhythm. When the encourager and customer are in harmony with their beliefs, their feelings or their actions, they are in the agreement mode. The encourager is sensitive to offer new information in such a way that initially highlights their points of agreement. The sales pro makes sure that the mood is always, *"we agree on mostly everything."* For example, when hearing an objection that suggests that the encourager and the customer are in a disagreement mode, the encourager starts by responding with the word, *"And…."* rather then with the word, *"But…."*

Why? *"And"* keeps the customer's head nodding in agreement, while, "But," cues disagreement, and puts the customer on the alert to defend her original position.

Customer: *"This cost is much higher than we originally talked about."*

***Salesperson**:* "**But** (subtle disagreement) *look at the extra features you are getting."*

Customer: *"**But*** (disagreement) *this is not the price you gave me before."*

Or

Customer: *"This cost is much high than we originally talked about."*

Salesperson: "**And** (subtle agreement) *look at the extra features you are getting."*

***Salesperson**:* (Silence, processing) *perhaps concluding, "We are not really that far apart, I guess our disagreement is not that strong."*

- Keep the theme that, "seems like we agree on mostly everything."
- Look for areas of agreement, even in points of disagreement.
- Sense common interests, experiences.
- Identify common strengths.
- Notice common ways of thinking.
- Highlight and emphasize areas of agreement.
- Stay tuned to being on the same side with your customer.
- Be sensitive to moments in which you begin experiencing each other as being on opposite sides, and quickly re-route to avoid entering the disagreement mode.
- *"Why this product is perfect for you"* (Instead of convincing him that his needs are wrong).
- Always (absolute word, remember?) replace the word *"but"* with the word *"and"* in selling.
- And never play devil's advocate again!

7 ANXIOUS RESISTANCE

"Take the uncertainty away from the anxious buyer"

- Where have you had anxiety resistance and eventually bought something and had a great experience with that product? Use your example if appropriate.
- Where might you employ overcoming anxiety resistances?
- Use absolute words with the anxious resistor when you believe the words are accurate.
- Focus on the benefits, the positive outcome of using your product.
- Offer guarantees.
- Reassure by communicating your accessibility.
- Offer testimonials of previous clients who had the same feelings she has, and today are happy with this product

A customer with an anxiety resistance isn't buying your product because he is experiencing too many uncertainties. He has doubts, some of which he can't even identify. Something isn't right or something could go wrong with the product. We experience anxiety when we are living in an uncertain state. The anxious customer tends to conclude in her uncertainty that buying the product will result in negative consequences.

"I'm a little nervous about trying that new hairstyle because I just don't know how it will look on me."

In the above statement, the customer is not taking on a newer look because she just doesn't know. Not knowing is scary. She's uncertain, and it probably won't look good. So to avoid the negative or painful outcome, and the anxious feelings associated with making the decision, the customer retreats to the known and safe way of doing things in the past. The known. The predictable. Keep the same hairstyle.

The encouraging sales person is at her best with the customer experiencing anxious resistance. When an encourager recognizes that the customer is experiencing uncertainty (anxiousness), the encourager knows that anxiousness is not necessarily bad, it is just uncertain. Going through our comfort zone from the safety, security and predictability of the past into the treasures of the unknown involves risking. But hasn't every great achievement in our lives been preceded by this period of anxiousness?

If we focus on the negative outcome of uncertainty, we give up.

"I might strike out if I go to bat" or in buying, thinking *"Maybe this product won't work"*

However if we focus on the positive outcome of uncertainty, we go forward.
"Going to bat is the only way I can hit a home run!" or in ***buying, thinking***
"Imagine how great it will be using this product"

8 ASKING EARLY IN THE SELLING PROCESS

Keep checking if it is ripe for closing time by asking questions that assume a close, and watch your customer's response.

Always keep in mind the possibility that the customer is ready to buy now. There are sensitive ways to take the customer's buying pulse. Checking *"Are we there yet?"* may help save you, and especially your customer valuable time. Because if you are there, you need not continue driving to get to the sale, or worse yet drive beyond and miss your destination.

Realtor: *"So you like the layout, and the location is in the area you desire. We are so lucky that this property came on the market on Tuesday. What are your reactions to the terms (leading up to asking early)?"*

Customer: *"The price strikes me as a little high."*

Realtor: *"What strikes you as a reasonable price on the property?"*

Customer: *"Oh, about thirty or thirty-five thousand dollars less, I'd say."*

Realtor: *"While this beautiful property in this great location is a new listing and you are the first one through, I'm not sure there is that much room, but you never know. Would you like to make an offer that can move you closer to taking ownership and taking it off the market (asking early)?"*

Asking early involves checking if the customer is ready to buy the product yet, or if more selling time is needed.

- Always be sensitive to the fact that the customer is ready to buy
- Certain questions can help early asking.
- *"Would you prefer green or blue?"*
- *"Would you like your products delivered this week or next?"* assumes the sale and shifts the focus on to the color or on to the delivery date.
- Develop and memorize some other examples of questions you can ask your customer early.
- *"What do you think?"*
- Be ready to sell a product quickly to the person who has researched the product and is here to buy it.

9 ASSET FOCUSING

"Focus on your customer's strengths, assets, resources, possibilities and potential to build him"

- Be one of the rare positive persons in your customer's life.
- Be obsessed with focusing on what's right with your customer, what's positive with him or her.
- Tune yourself in to your customer's claims-to-fames. Claims-to-fames are personal proud moments in your customers' lives when they achieved something. *"I once won...."*
- Customer has as is evidenced by their achievement.
- Be quick to give a compliment and notice positives that go over the head of others.
- Communicate your belief in people that they can do it.
- Identify one positive point about every customer you expect to meet today if you know who your customers will be.
- You can't pick people up by putting them down. The only way of lifting people up is to focus on their strengths
- If your customers are walk-ins, then observe something positive to say to them.
- What are some possible assets you can focus on with a customer today?
- Recall previous conversations in which your customer expressed her strengths or claims-to-fames to put the customer back into a positive mood. That is really customer service, isn't it?

Selling is encouraging. The best salespersons know how to encourage their customers to take advantage of the benefits they can get from their products. When I ask people what qualities the most encouraging people in their lives had, I consistently hear the same responses.

"My encourager believed in me, even more than I believed in myself."

"My encourager focused on what was right, rather than what was wrong with me."

Asset focusing involves talking about your customer's assets and strengths to focus your customer's attention on to her potential. Asset focusing is one of the most vital encouragement skills because talking about strengths gives the person's energy and lifts the person's spirits. Focusing on a person's assets centers attention to the resources the customer has to enhance her confidence and courage.

ASSOCIATING YOURSELF WITH POSITIVE FEELINGS 10

"Always be associated in your customer's mind as a good news giver" (Did you ever hear someone say, "here comes bad news?")

Did you ever hear a song playing in the background at the very moment you were having a powerful emotional experience? What happens when you hear that same song playing today? You probably re-live the emotions from your previous experience. The song and the experience are linked, or associated, in your mind.

The next time you are with a group of people, look for the uplifting person. The brightest human spot in the room. He is the one whose arrival lights up the atmosphere, who circulates good news, who mobilizes the resources of each person, and who conveys the energy giving optimism that raises the group *"will"* over the *"won't."* The line gathers waiting to be lifted by this human lighthouse. He is linked or associated with energy, joy, optimism and fun. He has earned this right because in the past he always brought a positive feeling into the experience.

The Law of Association concludes that when two events occur simultaneously, whether related or not, they are perceived as being linked, coupled or associated. If you have a friend who is always complaining, or bitter, the person's arrival triggers associated negative feelings in you. Perhaps you've heard the phrase, *"don't kill the messenger!"* That is because the messenger is linked or associated with the bad news and becomes the scapegoat.

By the same concept, customers tend to associate the feelings they are experiencing at any given moment with the person they are with, at that moment. Consequently customers, and most people, in fact, are naturally inclined to like the good news giver, and feel negative around the bad news giver. The encourager creates conditions to help the customer associate good feelings with his and his product's presence.

The Law of Association can be summarized as *"I see you = I feel great!"*

- Think of three feelings that you would like people to associate with you and to experience when they are with you.
- Be associated with being a good news giver to every customer you meet today.
- Be cautious about being associated with bad news, talking about internal business problems, fellow difficult employees or hassling the customer over a previous bill.
- Recognize that if you are having a bad day today and are living between happy hours, unless you start looking up, you could become associated with being a downer.
- Never complain to your customer about the traffic jam you went through to get to work or the customer's home.
- Never bring in personal problems during the sale to avoid becoming associated with problems.
- Have a joke, a compliment or a great way of looking at the day.

Agreement made

11 ASSOCIATED STATE

Encourage your customer to imagine herself experiencing the benefits of your product.

- List some states with which your product could be associated.
- Look at your product and let the scenes emerge.
- Connect the associated state with the customer's specific needs.
- To the customer with achievement needs, *"Can you picture yourself putting that new deck out in your backyard on a nice spring day dreaming of using it in the summer?"*
- To the customer with financial motivation needs, *"Can you feel the extra money in your pocket that you save from buying this equally effective product?"*
- To the person with security motivation needs, *"Can you image how safe you'll feel now that you have the top of the line product to protect you?"*
- Develop a few scenarios where you are using associated state by getting your customer to experience himself in the setting using your product.
- Engage as many of your customer's senses in the associated state.
- Add your customer's friends, relatives, or lovers that your customer talks about to her associated state.

Imagine it is possible, at this moment, to put yourself into any state you choose. New York? California? How about dreaming under the dancing palm trees in the state of Hawaii? Or maybe skiing on the snowy slopes in the state of Vermont? Well, you don't have to limit your states you can put yourself into by U.S. States. You can help to create emotional and motivational states of security, joy, bliss, serenity or even ecstasy. Any state you want, right there in your unlimited, creative mind.

An encourager puts a customer into an associated state by encouraging her to experience herself in a new state associated with your product.

"Picture yourself in your new home, in the living room in front of your crackling fireplace on a snowy day."

"Can you imagine yourself with this new look?"

"Super Bowl Sunday, you and your friends are watching the biggest game of the year on your new plasma TV. Can you see it? Doesn't get much better than that, does it?"

"Can you imagine yourself biting into this delicious Dove Bar with its rich chocolate, and creamy vanilla ice cream inside?"

ATTENTION TO PRODUCT DETAIL

12

Immerse your customer's senses into very specific details of your product.

Nobody does it better than a wine snob, do they? You watch him swirl the grape elixir in the glass, hold it up to the light, tip it down to see how many "legs" fall along the side of the glass, dip his nose into the glass to get a whiff of the bouquet, take a sip and swish it around the mouth as if gargling with Listerine, and then give approval or not.

Attention is the process by which the encourager makes some stimulus become sharper, clearer, more distinct, more vivid, more sensory to the customer. *"Stroke this fine Egyptian cotton sheet, 400 count. Can you imagine this feeling on your body?" Or... "Taste this warm cream cheese crab and artichoke dip with these Pennsylvania pretzels."*

Don't you want a Pennsylvania pretzel more than you want a pretzel? Or a Vidalia onion, rather than just any onion! Or French Champagne, Maine lobster, Carolina red tomatoes, Kansas City beef, and on and on?

- The adjective details add value to your product. Think of some of your products and new ways of describing them.
- City or country of origin, e.g. Persian carpets
- Think sharp.
- Think clear.
- Think distinct.
- Think details.
- Color details, especially if unusual.
- Scent, aroma details.
- Visual appeal details.
- Tactile appeal details.
- Auditory appeal details.
- Cost details.
- Status earning details.

13 ATTENTION FOCUSING STATEMENTS

Grab your customer's attention with direct, sharp focusing words and phrases like, 'LOOK HERE NOW!'

A restaurant in Manhattan gets to the point fast with its sign, *"Eat Here Now!"* The what, where and when are embedded crisply in those three words. The sign is a clear call to action. No wasted words here. Sure its a little more wordy than Seinfeld's favorite restaurant, the generic *"Restaurant,"* but it grabs the customer's attention a little more effectively.

Attention focusing statements are phrases designed to grab the customer's full-undistracted focus. Some attention focusing statements are, *"look here now!" "If you remember only one thing from this moment, let it be,"* or *"tune into this like you have never tuned in before,"* or, *"grab your pen and get this down."*

Attention focusing statements make the product more vital to a person's life, more concrete and specific, more real, new, with elements of the familiar, closer to home with elements of surprise, humor or shock.

- Identify the most crucial benefit or point of your message.
- Develop a few attention focusing statements to describe your products.
- *"Lowest Cost Anywhere!"*
- *"Longest Lasting."*
- *"Highest Efficiency"*
- *"Watch this!"*
- Prepare your customer for the event—you are about to deliver your attention focusing statement.
- Write the sentence in big print.
- Message.
- Stand closer to your customer or sit up to bring attention to what you are about to say.
- Get the person to repeat.
- You can add urgency to your message with the word *"Now!" Remember, "Eat Here Now!"*

ATTITUDE MODIFICATION

14

You can start changing your customer's attitudes by changing either her beliefs, feelings or intended actions.

"I would have never, never in a million years pictured a gas fireplace in my home," she explained. *"Too plastic, no crackling sounds, no scent from the woods."*

"But," she went on, *"the salesman flicked on the showroom switch and my fireplace is on. He told me that my time would be better spent stirring my drink and preparing my hors d'oeuvres. That made me think. After visiting me, many of my snobby friends have caved in as well! No more carrying wood in on freezing days for any of us."*

When working with a resistant customer, both selling and encouraging often involve modifying a customer's sometimes long held attitudes. When the customer buys a product she once said, *"no"* to, something took place to change the way she was thinking or feeling about the product. This change is often the result of the sales person's use of attitude modification. Every successful sales person wants to know how this attitude change occurred.

Attitudes are vital buying factors. In fact, psychologically speaking, we are our attitudes. What is an attitude? Attitudes are composed of three factors; (1) our beliefs or thoughts, (2) our emotions or feelings, and (3) our behaviors, actions or our intended actions. Attitude modification then, is any significant change in a customer's beliefs, feelings and actions. Positive attitude modification is frequently the result of encouragement.

The customer's attitude is composed of thoughts, emotions and actions. The sales encourager employ three specific tools of influence; (1) a logical approach to the customer who buys using words like, *"I think,"* or *"that makes sense,"* (2) an emotional presentation to the customer who says, *"I feel,"* or *"it feels right"* and (3) action words for the one who talks about doing, *"getting things done,"* or *"taking action."*

Attitude modification involves changing all three of these components, usually by changing your customer's strongest one first.

- Remember: Attitude = Beliefs or Thoughts + Emotions + Actions
- Believers or thinkers are moved primarily by logic.
- Use numbers and charts with believers, thinkers.
- Feelers are inspired by emotional appeals.
- Use feeling words with excitement for feelers.
- Doers change their attitude with messages encouraging them to *"take action now!"*
- Employ action words with doers.
- When your customer changes her attitude, isolate which of the three tools was most effective in causing that attitude change. This will reveal to you the most effective approach to attitude modification in the future.

15 ATTRACTIVENESS (PSYCHOLOGICAL)

Look your best, feel your best, show that smile, have a compliment, be light to lift and have something to offer your customer.

- Look your best, feel your best, be your best
- Communicate your liking for your customer
- Focus on the beliefs, values and attitudes you share with your customer
- Be easy and fun to be with
- Be real, genuine and share a little about yourself when it fits in with the conversation
- Bring humor and occasional reflections of your imperfections
- Help your customer feel unified with you in some way, some cause, or some purpose
- Have something to offer your customer
- What are some other ways for you to increase your psychological attractiveness?

Psychological attractiveness is having qualities that appeal to the customer. Physical attractiveness is a part of the total picture of psychological attractiveness, and is helpful in the initial phases of the selling relationship. Someone who is perceived as attractive buy another is more rewarding to be with. So physical attractiveness can help, but it needs to be backed up with other qualities, as well.

In addition to physical attractiveness, psychological attractiveness is associated with charisma, to intellectual and emotional stimulation, to authority, power and strength, and even to honesty, realness and vulnerability.

Social psychologists Bertram Ravin and Jeffrey Rubin have identified a number of reasons why we like others and find them attractive:

• We like a person's personal characteristics or traits.

• We are attracted to a person who we feel unified with or who we can identify with.

• We are attracted to a person who we perceive likes us.

• We like a person who offers us some material benefits.

• We are attracted to the person with whom we feel comfortable.

Most studies in social psychology have revealed that the more people share our beliefs, attitudes and values, the more attractive they become to us. We also tend to like people who we perceive think highly of us, and people like people who agree with them.

In addition. the more psychologically appealing the encourager, the more persuasive potential the person has. *Psychological Attractiveness = Persuasiveness*

AUDITORY BIAS

16

Sell auditory customers through your well-chosen words.

Some people are right handed and some people are left-handed. Some people are believers, thinkers and some people are feelers. And some people have auditory, while others have visual or kinesthetic representational styles. What does that mean?

Our representational style is the primary sense we most frequently use to represent the world to ourselves. A visual person primarily represents the world to himself in pictures and images (visual bias), while an auditory person represents the world to himself through words and sounds (auditory bias).

How do you recognize an auditory customer? A customer with an auditory bias is most effectively encouraged or discouraged by words. Words and sounds stimulate auditory sensations in the customer's mind. The auditory person's highs and lows are related to sounds. The auditory person has a stronger reaction to loud sounds or disharmonious words and auditory distractions, than others. **Auditories** are the first ones to hear a sound in the background and ask, *"Did you hear that?"* They also love the words and melody of the music in the background and are moved by romantic words in a song or a lover's soft voice.

Select your words wisely when making a presentation to an auditory customer. For example, words or phrases like, *"listen, hear, harmonize, tune in, clear as a bell, loud and clear,"* appeal to a customer with an auditory bias. And when a customer tells you that your idea, *"Sounds good,"* or he says, *"I hear you,"* you know that you are with an auditory person.

Prepare your presentation in a way that appeals to a customer with this auditory bias. For example, it wouldn't be as effective if you'd present your product with the words, *"See what I mean,"* because that would connect to a visual biased person.

- Practice listening for customers who have an auditory bias. They love words, sounds, music, and would rather listen to a tape than read a book.
- An auditory person's speech is slow, organized and clear and articulate.
- During your presentation ask, *"Do you hear me?"* or *"Does that sound about right?"*
- Speak with rhythm, because a monotone voice turns an auditory off.
- Use alliteration whenever possible. Alliteration creates a nice melody by offering a few words in a sentence that start off with the same sounds, e.g. *"shiny shoes, butter biscuits, etc."*
- Keep your ear to the ground and listen for customers with an auditory bias
- Does any of this ring true to you?
- An auditory customer experiences a freezing silence in the background of a restaurant or beauty salon hat isn't playing music.
- *"Can't wait to hear from you?"* and *"Sounds good!"* are typical auditory phrases.

17 AUTHORITY

Tactfully reveal your experiences, knowledge, training and expertise in areas that will be helpful to your customer.

- Be an expert on the history of your company. Spend time learning about who founded your company and why he or she was motivated to build your company.
- Capture the original passion for the purpose of your company.
- Share your company's mission or vision statement with your customer.
- Become an expert on your customer's company if he or she is a buyer or user of your product.
- Reveal your expertise and awareness of your customer's struggles.
- Be an authority in your field. Know everything you can about your competitor
- Look like an expert without overdoing it. Ask yourself, *"What does an expert look like in my field?"*
- Communicate your experience in the business, the number of years, your education and training, seminars you attended, etc.
- Learn everything you can about your product's strengths and communicate your knowledge.
- Talk about *"what's new,"* revealing that you are tuned into the-state-of-the-art in your business.
- Prefer showing, rather than telling, what you know.
- How else can you subtly increase your authority with your customers?

In general, a person who is perceived as being an authority (through title, dress, actions, achievements, knowledge, etc.) has more encourager potential on the customer. The customer's beliefs, feelings and actions are more likely going to be modified if the encourager is accepted as a legitimate authority.

An encourager subtly communicates authority through manners, dress, empathy for the customer's concerns and previous experiences, knowledge and personal positioning, e.g., *"I've been in business at this same location for over nine years."*

A solid way of becoming an authority is to learn everything you can about the features and benefits of your products, the advantages of your products over others, the cost and quality of your products as well as the stock and delivery time. And of course, the financing and billing arrangements for your customers.

Never forget that you are an expert on your product because you are selling it for a living. Never assume that a customer knows as much as you know about your product. Even though you make anywhere from one to dozens of sales presentations each day, the customer in front of you is hearing your presentation for the first time. You are the authority on your product. As a sales encourager, you are also an expert in understanding how to satisfy your customer's needs, as well.

BALANCE

18

Connect your product to your customer without violating her values and opinions.

Did you ever try to feed a duck, or tougher yet, an egret or a pelican? If so you learned about balance. You have to approach the winged animal very, very slowly and deliberately. One move too fast throws the relationship off balance and off the bird goes into the wild blue yonder. Or have you ever seen a conservative convince a liberal or vice versa, in one discussion? Probably not. Because of balance.

Psychological balance is the human tendency to quickly accept smooth flowing, calmly positioned consistent, compatible beliefs and to just as quickly reject shoving, inconsistent, incompatible ones. An encourager respects the beliefs, feelings and actions of the customer knowing the customer will be forced to defend their previous beliefs if attacked. And the sales person doesn't want the customer spending energies defending, and further reinforcing past decisions to buy from the competitor, do they?

So the encourager is sensitive to start in the agreement mode and to offer new ideas, slowly and palatably that allow the balance to be modified in doses that the customer will accept.

- Someone is using your competitor's product. Ask yourself if she is using it for its cost, quality or concept advantage. If they have an emotional or logical connection to the product, respect the fact that you are taking her off-balance (and may create the boomerang effect).
- Sell your product by tying your product in a way that balances your customer even better than the current product.
- To move a person from product 1 (least expensive) to product 10 (most expensive), progress to 2,3, etc. (Curiously I just opened up a fortune cookie which read, "Two small steps is sometimes better than one big leap!")
- Once you know a customer's belief, keep the person as on balance as possible by communicating, *"I thought of you when I saw this product, because it is just what you believe in."*

19 BEHAVIORAL CONTAGION

Show how your product is "on the move" and "on fire!

Matrix's professional beauty line of Biolage products took off immediately and became the all time beauty industry winner. Customers love Biolage and support it by purchasing the whole line. Almost every salon in North America sells Biolage. Biolage is contagious with good, clean feelings.

Many other products, like the first Ford Mustangs in its time, and today's Starbucks, and Canada's Tim Horton Doughnuts all experienced and are continuing to experience behavior contagion. When you hear that this product is *"hot," "on the move,"* or *"flying off the shelves,"* a behavioral buying contagion is occurring.

Products, like smiles, can be contagious, and are often passed from one person to another. The stock market crash of 1929 was the result of a negative behavioral contagion when everyone started withdrawing their money from their banks at once. More recently in the toy market, we witnessed a behavior contagion with the toys of the year ranging from Cabbage Patch Dolls, Furbies, Pokemon, and on and on.

Behavioral contagion occurs when a customer, who is in conflict about trying something new, sees others trying it. The person's fears and anxieties are reduced and the customer becomes more willing to go for the new idea or product due to the behavioral contagion.

- Use examples, video, verbal, etc., of people who tried the new idea or product and found positive results. The new idea or product can become contagious thus stirring momentum.
- How can your dealership, distributorship, store or business start the momentum?
- Create a behavioral contagion strategy for one of your products.
- Help each other as salespersons talking up the trend to each other's customers, *"My customers are telling me that the key lime pie is awesome tonight"*
- Remember to use the absolute words from earlier in this book.

BELIEVABILITY

Earn credibility by being trustworthy and communicating your knowledge.

20

The sales person has to work hard at the small things to build big trust and earn believability. Building trust is actually relatively easy, if the encourager is committed to doing it right. Think about it. Who do people trust? People trust others who, in their past, simply did what they said they would do and had it done by the time they said it would be done. Believability is the customer's perception that the encourager's message is accurate, and can be counted on. Believability is credibility, and is a product of trustworthiness plus knowledge.

Trust is also helped by the sales person using a little self-disclosing. Self-disclosing involves sharing something about oneself that reveals a little about the person of the salesman. The self-disclosing needs to be honest, relevant and appropriate, and ideally may be a little humorous about one's own foibles. Self-disclosure and openness on the part of one person tends to follow with a little self-disclosure on the part of the other.

In addition to doing what you said you would do, share a little about yourself with your customer.

- Believability = Trustworthiness + Knowledge
- Create opportunities for you to show your customer that you do what you said you would. *"Hello, Mrs. Jones, I'll be with you in a few seconds as soon as I finish writing this message." Write the message, smile and remind her, thank you for your patience for those few seconds, and how may I help you today?"*
- Softly remind your customer that you did what you said you would that time. And will the next time, as well.
- Set up a time for a future call you will make to your customer. Be specific about the time you will call. *"Mrs. Kline, when is a convenient time for me to call you next week to hear about your husband's reactions to your highlights?" "Ok, I'll call you at exactly nine o'clock on Tuesday morning."*
- *"By four o'clock, I will have all of your closing costs detailed to the penny for next Monday's closing. May I call you immediately at four, or would another time be better for you, Mr. Key?"*
- Communicate your knowledge and accuracy by being as detailed as possible. If you worry about the details, and your customer notices your concern with details, she doesn't have to be worried herself.
- Do what you say you will do. Promise a customer something and deliver at exactly that time. This will help you establish your believability.
- Return anything you ever borrow.
- When relevant and when it fits into the conversation share a little honest comment, story or experience about yourself.
- Remember, self-disclosure on the part of the sales person leads to self-disclosure on the part of the customer. Self-disclosure builds trust and believability.

21 BODY ACCESSIBILITY

- You're an experienced sales pro in life. Close your eyes for a minute and picture a person's body language in a closed, and resisting state. What does it look like? Describe it to yourself for a few moments.
- Now picture this same person opening up. What changes are you seeing in this person's body language? Visualize signs of open body accessibility and contrast these signs with closed body accessibility. Cultivate your sensitivity to both.
- Rate a totally closed body accessibility as a *"1,"* and a totally open body accessibility as a *"10."* Visualize a person going from 10 to 1.
- Now visualize a person going from 1 to 10.
- Cultivate your sensitivity to the direction, opening up or closing down, at any moment in the selling process.

Study your customer's open or closed body language.

Walk by a classroom of students and look in the small windows at the class. You can tell, by the children's body language whether they are engaged in the topic or not. Picture a sales presentation with a group of people and, without hearing a word and just observing the prospective customers in the audience, you can tell immediately whether they are interested or not. One of the major cues you observe is the students, or the listening customer's body accessibility.

Body accessibility is the openness of a person, communicated through one's body, and is a leading clue to a person's readiness to buy. A customer whose body accessibility is closed is observed with arms folded across his chest, his legs are tightly shut and often his body is turned slightly to the left or the right. Even his mouth is shut. A person with a closed body accessibility is saying, *"I am not letting these ideas in. I'm closed!"*

Contrarily, a person with an open body accessibility has open arms, sits up or stands a little closer, is direct, and is nodding his head. He is ready to let the new ideas in. The encourager constantly observes what specific ideas open or close a person's body accessibility.

The aware salesman notes, *"When I talked about the five year warranty the customer opened up, but when I said it only came in one color, the customer seemed to shut down."*

22

BOOMERANG EFFECT

Spot signs that your customer is suddenly changing his mind because maybe something that you said suddenly backfired (Boomerang!).

A boomerang, as we all know, is a toy, weapon or a game that you throw outward, and it is designed to return to the thrower. Boomerangs are great everywhere, everywhere but in selling. The boomerang effect is happening when the customer starts to change her mind in the opposite direction desired by the encourager. The encourager is constantly sensitive to the behaviors, e.g. a customer's words, body accessibility and major shifts in the customer's reactions. The encourager realizes that boomerang is always the result of some causes.

Customer: *"What do you mean write out a check for $3100. I thought you said the cruise was $1300 per person. Two persons are $2600."*

Travel agent: *"Yes, but you have taxes and port fees and miscellaneous costs."*

Customer: *"Forget it." (Boomerang!)*

Accurately analyzing and addressing the boomerang can save a sale. And many future sales may be saved as well, since the boomeranging customer builds up anger at the salesman, the business or the product.

Customer: *"I saw your sign that you have Old Reading Beer for only $15.00 a case. Give me 3 cases."*

Salesman (brings out 3 cases): *"That's 45.00 plus tax"*

Customer: *"Wait, these are only 7 ounce, not 12 ounce bottles!"*

Salesman: *"Yeah, you couldn't expect to get Old Reading, 12 ounces for $15.00."*

Customer: *"But your sign doesn't say that these are just 7 ounces."*

Salesman: *"The sign didn't say 12 ounces, did it?"*

Customer: *"I'm out of here!" (Boomerang!)*

Ever happen to you?

- Recall a time you experienced the boomerang effect as a customer yourself. What caused the boomerang? How could it have been avoided?
- Recall sales presentations that you gave that produced boomerang. As you analyze the message, what was the source of the boomerang?
- Be sensitive to times when the customer boomeranged, but never said a word. Since most customers never complain, but just never returned, boomerang is more common than we are aware.
- When a customer whose body language was once open and is now closed down, chances are it was the result of the boomerang effect. Sensitively address your observation with a non-judgmental subtle question such as, *"What is your reaction to the payment plan?" "Warranty?" "Quality?" " Cost?"*
- No surprises at closing time, unless they are positive ones.

23 BUYING SIGNS

Notice your customer nodding, coming closer, looking at sales brochures, asking questions, talking about price or delivery time.

When the line outside the store is a block long waiting for the doors to open with the newly arrived truckload for today's equivalent of Beanie Babies, everyone recognizes the waiting as a buying sign. But how do you identify buying signs on your everyday customers? What are buying signs anyway? Buying signs are the verbal and non-verbal hints and cues that the buyer gives to the seller.

Buying signs vary from personality to personality, as some people are more expressive than others, and some people are non-conscious, and others are conscious resistors. For example when I am enthused about a product, my buying signs are always visible. Unfortunately, this is disadvantageous to me. When my friend and I buy a beach property that we rent out rent during the summer, George is tough on the Realtor. George is the tire kicker, the head shaker who can't believe this atrocious price, the horrible condition of the house, the repair costs, the carpet condition and the thin walls. And yes, while he will agree with the agent that the property has one of the finest views in Ocean City Maryland, he quickly adds, *"and it looks like a hurricane magnet!"* So during the time George is testing the water pressure, I'm sitting on the oceanfront porch listening to my CD of Chris Cross's song, *"Sailing, takes me away!"*

And curiously George wants the property for our families and for renters as much as I do. George has different buying signs. You just have to look closer. What are some common buying signs?

- The key buying sign is the customer's investment of time, effort and energy. A shrewd salesperson, for example, would recognize that George is investing much energy and time into his criticism of the beach property. Why would he take his valuable time unless he was interested?
- The more questions the customer asks, the more interest the customer has.
- The more difficult the question the customer asks, the more the customer is a conscious, rather than a non-conscious resistor. And that is good news for you because you are dealing with up front objections.
- Another buying sign is that the customer leans towards you or your product.
- The customer picking up or using the product indicates interest.
- The customer encouraging her family to use the product suggests that she is sold.
- The customer talking about delivery time is indicating intense interest.
- The customer discussing different colors is picturing herself as the product owner, in her context.
- Add some buying signs that you have observed.

CATHARSIS

24

Be a safe place for your customer to vent her emotions.

A tattooed sailor man named Popeye explained it the best with his immortal words, "Dats all I can stands, I can't stands no more!" Were you ever so angry at the service you received at a business or the department of motor vehicles, that you just lost it? Most of my personal scenarios of being emotionally challenged occurred at airports. When you re-live your frustration and anger, venting still almost makes sense to you, doesn't it? By the same token, to the customer who is letting it all out, her behavior is making sense to her because she believes no one is listening and no one really cares, and I have no where else to turn. This is a cathartic moment.

You have experienced catharsis watching a movie with the patient on the psychiatrist's couch letting it all out. Or you've seen catharsis with the suspect on the stand in the court braking down under tough questioning.

In selling, catharsis is occurring when the customer is intensely expressing his emotions. Catharsis is the venting of a person's real feelings, which may or may not be consistent with the encourager's feelings. When the encourager allows the customer's catharsis or venting of their attitude, especially their hostile feelings first, the air becomes cleaner, objections surface, and the customer becomes more willing to then listen to the encourager's message. Encouragers care. Encouragers want to hear the customer's frustrations, anger, feelings and objections.

The encourager is cautious to allow a one time venting, and responds, *"You told me that before and I heard you,"* when the customer wants to go on and on. This prevents the customer from re-experiencing and hearing his own story again, creating further anger and possibly, yes, the boomerang effect.

- Care. Imagine when you had emotional moments such as your customer is having now.
- Initially don't expect your customer to be reasonable. The person's levels of emotions are high and are not cured by reason very easily.
- Understand your customer's feelings when he is venting his anger or frustration.
- During the customer's catharsis, avoid the natural tendency to interrupt, or correct the person. Allow the person full expression. Listen carefully.
- Experience your customer's anger as, not anger, but hurt. When you sense the hurt, rather than the anger in the complaining client, how do you relate differently?
- Share back the feelings you heard your customer express.
- Think of a time a customer went into a catharsis mode with you. How could you handle it most effectively?

25 CHANNELS OF COMMUNICATION

- What channels of communication do you currently use?
- How can you increase your channels of communication and appeal to more of the sensory and attitude biases of your customers?
- How does your message appeal to the visual person who needs to see it?
- How does your message appeal to the auditory person who needs to hear it?
- How does your message appeal to the kinesthetic person who needs to touch and interact with your product?
- How does your message appeal to the thinker who needs logic and reason, benefits and features?
- How does your message appeal to the feeler who needs to be moved by it?
- Develop creative ways for your customer to use or to interact with your message.
- When presenting to a group, use as many channels of communication as possible to connect to the different styles and personalities in the room.

Communicate your message, not only through your words, but use sales tools, inspiring videos and any other channels of communication.

The **channels of communication** are the specific vehicles with which the message is delivered. These may include face-to-face, print, video, or audio, etc. An encourager uses a variety of channels of communication that appeal to the sensory bias (visual, auditory) and the attitude bias (belief, feeling or intended action) of the customer.

CHARISMA

26

Look up, eyes wide open, bring enthusiasm to your words, let your arms reach out, because you have something important for your customer.

President Kennedy had it! Michael Jordan still has it! Most great leaders have it. Charisma. And probably your high school class president and class representatives had it. Charisma. The person with charisma often has leadership qualities.

While, unfortunately some charismatic leaders manipulated their people for power, fame or money, the charismatic leader's work can change the world in positive ways. Ghandi, Martin Luther King, Pope John Paul, Mother Theresa and The Dahli Lama, each made the world a better place through their charisma and their commitment to building a better world.

Charisma is the degree of magnetism, charm or enthusiasm a person has. In selling, the charismatic salesperson brings magnetism, charm and enthusiasm towards the product. Charisma adds value. Charisma may be upbeat, outgoing rah, rah, or charisma may be a soft, but strong and sure demeanor.

Encouragers with charisma communicate by lighting up their message with enthusiasm. Why? Because charismatic sales professionals have a passion. A passion for the product. A passion for people. And a passion for selling. The charismatic salesperson believes that *"our ideas and our products are important and can improve your life!"*

- If you don't believe you have charisma, what if you acted like you did?
- How would you act if you had more charisma?
- How would you look if you had more charisma?
- How would you relate to your product if you had more charisma?
- How would you relate to your customer if you had more charisma?
- For which of your products do you have the most passion?
- What can make you passionate about in your work in selling?
- Which of your products can you develop your charisma over most effectively?
- Come to life!
- Bring your products to life! Charismatize them!

27 CLOSING

Close the sale! Score! Getting runners to third base doesn't count.

- Make your goal closing the sale. Remember, many baseball teams can get runners on bases, but the runs do not count until they reach home, or until the team closes the sale.
- Use silence wisely. Sense if the customer is moving in the direction of buying or not. If moving away from buying, gently encourage the customer with the benefits important to her.
- Offer no surprises at closing. Make sure that the customer is aware of all the extra costs, taxes, etc. prior to closing.
- Offer a small gift for big purchases at closing.
- Communicate your accessibility. Do not leave your customer before, during or soon after the closing.

The closing is the moment of the customer takes action and buys. The closing may have been caused by the encourager's words or even, the encourager's *"way of being in the relationship."* Something has happened that moved the customer from, *"no,"* or *"not sure"* to *"yes."* The more that the salesperson knows what that something is, the more that needs to be focused on, repeated and reinforced. Straying from that fact that made the difference can be detrimental to the sale, and the customer may lose the product because the salesperson shifted topics at the moment of closing.

Being quiet may be a valuable tool if wisely used at the close. Sense which direction the customer's momentum is going, towards buying or towards leaving. The more the customer is moving towards buying, allow him a short processing period through your silence, with only an occasional reminder of the benefits. The more the customer appears to be moving away from the sale, the more encouragement is helpful. If you truly believe that your customer can benefit from your product.

Encouragement's goal is the closing. When the encouraging coach sees the team pull off that perfect play to win the game, that is the closing sought. When the encouraging sales professionals hears, *"yes,"* from the customer, that is the closing. Call it a game at that point, and avoid the possible loss in extra innings!

COMMITMENT

28

Get your customer to make a public commitment to owning your product by a certain point in the future.

Weight loss programs are the best at getting a commitment. In some programs, participants tell the group their goal, and or they write their goal down and make a commitment to achieving the goal. The goal becomes the support group and the encouragers commitment to each other. Some of the encouragers are there for the weigh in and the cheers, applause, encouragement and support overflows. The commitment, made in public, puts a great deal more incentive into the participants drive to improve or be better.

Commitment is encouraged when the saleswoman (1) gets a person to take some action consistent with his or her attitude or values, (2) suggests the person make her attitude public, and (3) helps a person sense that her attitudes are irrevocable.

Many commitments are quantifiable and are connected by deadlines, dates and numbers. This way these goals are verifiable and not tenuous, uncertain or *"iffy."*

- Make your goal closing the sale. Remember, many baseball teams can get runners on bases, but the runs do not count until they reach home, or until the team closes the sale.
- Use silence wisely. Sense if the customer is moving in the direction of buying or not. If moving away from buying, gently encourage the customer with the benefits important to her.
- Offer no surprises at closing. Make sure that the customer is aware of all the extra costs, taxes, etc. prior to closing.
- Offer a small gift for big purchases at closing.
- Communicate your accessibility. Do not leave your customer before, during or soon after the closing.

29 CONGRUENCE

Let your body language be a big supporter of your words.

- To develop your congruence, practice your sales presentation a few times without the benefit of words. In other words, let your body do the total talking and communicating your message without saying a word. Make your body's resources, your eyes, hand motions, etc. communicate your ideas. Tell the whole story through your body. Instead of saying, *"I feel strongly about this product"* let your hands, arms, eyes, and deliver the message. It will feel very awkward the first time, but each time you will get better at it. After practicing four or five times, then practice using your words with you non-verbal body language enhancing your words and putting yourself into a congruent state.
- Communicate congruency in all of your conversations throughout the day, even with family and friends. Make congruency a part of your life.
- Don't allow your message to lose its flow by creating interfering blocks between you and your customer.

When a customer starts doubting or distrusting a message's truth, it is often the result of the salesperson appearing incongruent. Incongruency is experienced when a person's words don't match, or aren't congruent, with the person's body language. When a person argues, *"I am not angry,"* while pounding his hand on the desk, he is being incongruent.

When a salesman says, *"this product is tremendous,"* while saying it in a monotone and standing with boring body language, he is in an incongruent state. When someone gets "bad vibes" from another, sometimes incongruency is the source. Lawyers study directly the demeanor of the witness, while the jury goes by its *"guts,"* as they view the juror's words and body language.

The salesperson who, despite being sincere and honest, but isn't congruent will lose sales that she could have won just by understanding and developing her *"way of being"* in a more congruent way, thereby delivering an accurate message.

Congruence is being achieved when a person's verbal and non-verbal actions synergize.

CONSCIOUS OR NON-CONSCIOUS RESISTANCE?

30

Understand whether your customer knows, or isn't aware of his objections for not buying.

Whatever you are thinking of at this moment is in your conscious mind. You are conscious of your current thoughts. Being conscious is being aware. When a customer consciously resists a new idea, he is able and capable of stating his resistance. Conscious resistances are easy to address, because the encourager knows the true reason behind the, "*no*!" The task of the encourager is to simply overcome the conscious resistance with new beliefs that offer benefits that overcome the conscious resistance.

Whatever you are not thinking of now is in your non-conscious mind. The non-conscious mind has two components. First, in your subconscious mind lives experiences and material that can be brought forth with a little effort, such as what you did on your last birthday. Secondly, in your unconscious mind exists material and experiences that are repressed or are unable to be brought forth. This material is revealed in dreams, and slips of the tongue.

Non-conscious resistances are those that the customer cannot identify why he isn't going to buy.

- Work at analyzing the true reason for a customer's objection. When a person knows why he is not buying and tells you why he is not buying, you avoid the pitfall of dealing with inaccurate or unconscious resistances.
- When your customer's resistance is conscious, ask, *"If it weren't for..., would you then consider our product?"*
- When your customer's resistance is non-conscious, create an atmosphere of honesty through your caring, empathy, warmth and respect while asking open-ended questions.
- Non-conscious resistances may be uncovered by the sensitive sales person: *"Perhaps the last time you made a big purchase you had problems and are thinking that big purchases equal problems. If so, I can understand that reasoning. That's why we are offering this guarantee and a smaller monthly payment plan."*

31 CONSISTENCY NEEDS (CUSTOMER)

Sell reliability and predictability to your customer with consistency needs.

- Be sensitive to customers who have consistency needs and like doing things the way they have always done them.
- If your customer always buys the same product, "I'd never buy anything but a Volkswagon!" find out what features are in a Volkswagon that he values. Determine if you can offer some of those same features.
- Be very sensitive about shifting the customer with consistency needs from one sales person to another. When Carol Kline is handling your Mortgage at Wachovia Bank, you won't be dealing with ten other people, having to rebuild rapport and trust ten different times.
- If the person with consistency needs is not using your product and tells you that he has used your competitor's product for years, do not be discouraged. See this as an opportunity. If you can win him over, he will now be just as loyal to you, and it will be difficult for someone else to win him over. In this way, a person with consistency needs can be a long-term treasure to win over.

All in the Family's Archie Bunker didn't like change. Not just changes in society, but any kind of change. He always sat in the same chair, ate the same foods, drank at the same bar and saw the world in a clear cut, black and white way. Archie had consistency needs.

A person with consistency needs is motivated by things that are reliable, predictable and will give order in her life. When something isn't predictable, guaranteed or certain, anxiety surfaces. Hence we observe the source of the anxious resister. The steady, stable predictable sales person arrives on time, or is ready at the appointment time for the customer seeking consistency needs. And if the sales person has any surprises, let the best surprise be an even more predictable product or service. Holiday Inn promised, "*The Best Surprise is No Surprise*!" Customers with consistency needs loved it.

An encourager couples the product in a way that it fulfills the customer's consistency needs. A person with consistency needs likes to vacation at the same places, eat at the same restaurants, and tends to be loyal to a certain product line. And to the same customer.

32

CONTRAST PRINCIPLE

Show an overpriced product prior to showcasing your product.

Salesperson: *"This suit is $750.00! You've got to be kidding!"*

Customer: *"How much is this one?"*

Salesperson: *"That's $375.00!"*

Customer: *"Well I like the $375 suit better than the $750 one."*

Salesperson: *"I'm sure we have it in your size would you like to try this one on?"*

Customer: *"Sure."*

The $375.00 suit was worth $375. However, the suit gained more value because in relation to the $750 suit it looked like a great bargain. How the value of the suit was increased is best explained by the contrast principle.

The contrast principle argues that a customer perceives things differently based upon the sequence in which the encourager presents the ideas or products. If the second item is fairly different than the first, we will tend to see it as more different than it actually is. For example, if we put our hand into a bucket of cold water first and lukewarm water second, we will perceive the lukewarm water to be warmer than it is. But, if we put our hand in warm water first, than into the same luke warm water, the lukewarm water will now appear to be colder than it is.

The first condition is the benchmark. The second product in then viewed, in relation to the first product. Real estate agents are adept at bench marking when they take a customer to a ridiculously priced house prior to taking them to the house that the customer might have an interest in and might have a reasonable chance of buying. The encourager uses the contrast principle to dramatically make a point of contrasting their idea in relation to another idea.

- How can you make use of the contrast principle?
- How can you vary the relative value of your product in relation to other products, other ways of using the same amount of money, the option of going through life without your product.
- Help your customer to be aware of the contrast to having this product he wants is to not have it.

33 COST RESISTANCE

Sell your customer who has a cost objection how your product will actually save her costs.

- Compare cost of big apples to big apples. Make sure your customer is aware of all of the factors that affect cost; size, durability, concentration, attractiveness, etc.
- Be cautious about bringing up the cost issue before your customer does.
- Keep your questions open and broad and allow your customer to bring up her resistance.
- Think of times you heard the cost resistance. Separate those times the cost resistance was the accurate, conscious reason for not buying from those times the cost resistance was just hiding another, truer non spoken resistance.
- Creating a safe atmosphere with your encouragement skills may help the customer feel comfortable to bring out the real resistance.

The question *"how much?"* may be a reflection of simple curiosity. Or it may suggest that the potential buyer is saying, *"Depending on the cost, I may buy."* Think about that. The buyer, possibly or probably, wants the product. The only issue is cost.

The cost resistance is heard in the words and phrases that vary from, *"That's a little high"* to the outright *"It costs too much."* The encourager can quickly read through the cost resistance statement for accuracy by simply asking the question, *"So if we could deliver this to you for less, then you would be interested?"* The cost resistance usually means, *"You haven't shown me enough benefits to buying your product."*

Be cautious about putting words or suggestions of high price into the mindset of the customer. For example, *"Does the price seem a little high to you?"* may cause the boomerang getting the customer to now focus on the high price.

A more effective, open-ended question allows the customer to bring out his own resistance without potentially adding another resistance.

"What are your reactions to the product?" Suppose the customer responds, *"Well, the price is too much,"* than it is time to do your selling. You found the resistance. Cost. The customer now needs to be shown more benefits.

"The price seems a little high to you? Let me explain what this product can do and I think that you'll see the nice advantages this product has that more than justify a few more dollars."

Occasionally the buyer is using the cost resistance to cover up another resistance. How can you tell? Well imagine that you offered the product at one-half the cost. If he wouldn't buy under those conditions, than the cost resistance wasn't the true objection.

COUPLING

34

Couple your newest product with a product that your customer previously had a positive experience.

"If you like Mounds bars, you'll love Almond Joy. An Almond Joy is a Mounds bar, plus almonds!"

"The car you've always loved, next year will be featured in a convertible. Your favorite car, plus top down!"

One of my publishers brought out a highly successful book called ***Think & Grow Rich***, and suggested the title of my manuscript be ***Think Your Way to Success!*** And then he could sell the new book by saying, *"**You Read Think & Grow Rich**. I introduce you to, **Think Your Way to Success!**"*

Coupling is riding the wave of a previous success. You might call coupling, "piggy backing." A great starting point to promote your new product is to couple it with a product that your customer had a previous positive experience with. This could be a product of yours or your competitors. Coupling enhances the already successful product, while minimizing the risk for the anxious and change resistor.

Another advantage of coupling is that you are applauding your customer's wise buying decisions in the past. Remember, never criticize a previous decision your customer made, because that is like calling him, "*stupid*," plus it forces him to defend and reinforce his previous decision. In coupling by applauding a past positive buying decision of your customers, you also are putting the two of you into an agreement mode.

Coupling involves linking, or associating, your product with the customer's conscious or non-conscious needs.

- Study your customer's favorite products. This observation will teach you many things about your customer. She selected these products for a reason.
- Identify products you have that are similar to the previous products your customer has chosen.
- Couple the customer's current product, with your product, and use the word, "*Plus*," to give your product that additional advantage.
- Coupling is consistent with your customer's beliefs, keeping her in balance.
- Coupling is helping your customer to take a previous proven winner, no risk, and adapting higher.
- Coupling may be used in another way. Couple your product with your customer's needs.
- First, study the customer's needs, e.g. Achievement, Quality, Cost, Etc.
- Couple your product's name in the same sentence as those needs.

35 CUSTOMIZING

Motivate your customer by telling him that you will design your product just for him

- Do you remember Burger King's at the time winning response to the mass produced burgers at McDonalds? Have it your way! Customized hamburger just for you.
- What are areas where your products and services may be customized?
- Customize yourself by being there for your customer at a time when you usually are not there. Of course, let the person know with a smile and a sincere, *"No problem, I'm here for you."*
- Communicate your willingness to customize your product whenever possible.
- Customizing may even involve delivering the product sooner than usual.

The store, *"Things Remembered"* figured it out. Imagine having your name on anything. Private labels appeal to those individuals who have what we will soon discuss as, ***"individuation needs."*** You will soon read about the individuals who value their uniqueness. They deserve special treatment! We all have a little bit of a need for individuation, don't we?

Why do so many people today, more than ever before crave customizing? In the 21st century, with increasing technology all around us, everywhere we go we are a number, aren't we? A license number, a social security number, a case number. In fact when I went to get my hair done a few years back, the stylist asked me, *"Are you my nine o'clock?"* I responded, *"No, I'm your customer!"* Kermit the Frog reflected on this isolation, alienation and feelings of insignificance when he concluded that its not that easy bein' green because everything around him was green and he lived in this thick green grass. He wished he could be sparkling or shining somewhere. Somebody give Kermit some customized service!

And I'm sure you've been frustrated by how long it takes you to speak with a human voice when you call a business. And what about those times when none of the prompts you hear relate to your own unique problem? One of the antidotes to this disease of insignificance is customizing.

Customizing involves making adaptations on a product to fit the specific needs of an individual customer. When a customer receives a customized treatment, he or she feels respected and important, and tends to develop even more of a loyalty to the business (and may be considered to offer testimonials). Customizing appeals extremely well to customers with dominance or individuation needs.

36

DESIRED PRODUCT QUALITIES

Ask your customer what her ideal product would look like and cost.

Nobody else could do it. No that's not quite true. Almost anybody else could do what Linda, the Chevy Cobalt salesperson did. She had our daughter dream of every feature she wanted on her first car. Color? OnStar? Sirius? CD? Sun Roof? Spoiler? Linda asked for a day to track exactly the desired product qualities. She even apologized asking if we could wait that long knowing how excited a 16 year-old is for her new car. Keep in mind that we had talked to four other salespersons prior to Linda who couldn't get everything our daughter desired. As you can guess, Linda made the sale. She was able to meet every desired product quality but one.

Maybe encouragers can't exactly do what priceline.com does when it allows the customer to name her own price for airline tickets, but the sales professional can encourage her customer to dream of the qualities of her desired product, and then get as close as possible to fulfilling the person's dreams.

Get your customer engaged in the selling process. Incidentally, our company created a few products based on what we learned from exploring our customer's ideal products. The encourager wants to know the ideal product qualities that the customer desires to learn more about the customer's needs and dreams, and maybe even a little about what your competitor is offering her.

- Learn about desired product qualities of the next new customer you meet. Then couple what the customer desires with those qualities, or some of those qualities with a product you currently offer, or customize whenever possible. And remember, when you encourage your customer to talk about her desired products qualities, the idea came from your customer who has now invested time in thinking about your product!
- Discuss the desired price range that your customer has in mind. Don't give up hope, even though you might have to help the person become realistic.

37 DISCOURAGED CUSTOMER

Sense the discouraged customer who likes and needs your product, but is still hesitant to buy.

Discouragement is in operation when a customer could benefit from the encourager's new ideas and products, but resists. The resistance may be the result of a variety of conscious or non-conscious reasons, and could be, relationship, or fact based. How many people could afford a better home, and would love to have one, but are discouraged and never live out their lives more fully? Because of discouragement? Discouragement limits who a person can be, what a person could achieve, what a person could have, because it is so much easier, and safer to keep things just as they are.

Encouragement selling focuses on helping people to overcome their own discouragement and experience life more fully. As Director of Admissions at a Pennsylvania Community College years ago, I would talk to waiters, waitresses, construction workers, and anyone I could asking them to stop by our college and learn how they may benefit from it. Most didn't come in, and those who did were often discouraged about *"going to college"* because of weak academic backgrounds or low self-esteem. My job was to sell them, encourage them to believe in themselves. Today, dozens of these once discouraged persons are teachers, sales professionals, business leaders, and a few are doctors, lawyers, a dentist, and one today a researcher with a Ph.D. looking for a cure for cancer. They were discouraged. The antidote is encouragement. They need to be sold by you.

- Identify the customers you have who could benefit from what you have to offer and you just can't get through. View the person as discouraged. The remedy is your encouragement. Help the person get more out of life.
- A person's self-image may hold him back from buying a new product. *"I'm not worth a $100.00 for pair of shoes."* An encourager recognizes the discouragement and helps the person get a new view of himself.
- Help your customer to never make the mistake of limiting the visions of their future by the narrow and limited experiences of their pasts.
- Encourage your customer to see himself as the person who he is in the process of becoming.

38

DISPLACEMENT

Recognize that your angry customer may be displacing his real anger at his wife, or another salesperson, on to you.

Remember The Three Stooges? Moe was the boss. As lead Stooge, Moe was in charge and at the top of the trio's pecking order. When Moe was upset or frustrated, he would turn to wild haired Larry and slap him. Larry would not dare slap Moe back so Larry would turn around and displace his frustration and anger on to the more helpless, rotund Curly. Curly would handle his frustration by rubbing his face a few times, and displace his emotions on to the floor as he shuffled his feet a few times. Larry and Curly were using displacement. They were displacing their feelings from one person on to another person or thing.

Displacement is directing a positive, or, more commonly, a negative emotion at someone other than the person to whom it was originally intended. The encourager is sensitive to the fact that the angry customer may really be angry at her husband, or even all men, and the encourager is the victim of the anger. The encourager recognizes the dynamics of displacement by asking oneself, *"Have I done something that could have caused this degree of anger?"* Through empathy, warmth and respect, and re-directing the anger to its original source through specific questions, the customer often will soften.

- Always consider that the upset customer has some unresolved problems from another context and is displacing those negative emotions on to you because, you are safe, you are understanding, and, you are there.
- Understanding displacement allows you to not take things personally. If the anger is continuous at you then you become assertive with the words, *"I'd like to talk with you, you seem upset with me, and I'd like to improve our relationship."*
- Also be aware of those times you may be displacing your anger from an argument with your spouse, sales manager, policeman or traffic jam on to your customer.

39 DIVORCING

Separate your new product from a previous product that your customer had a bad experience,

Divorcing is the opposite of coupling. Coupling is linking your new product with a previously successful product. Divorcing involves uncoupling false links that a customer has made in her mind between two products. The customer complains to her salesperson, *"I tried one of your products last year, and had a horrible experience."* In this instance the customer has made a generalized link, or coupled *"one of your products,"* with *"all of your products."*

The encourager divorces one product from another. *"I've had a few complaints about that product and understand what you are saying. That was frustrating (empathy). As you know our company has many successful products, for example, this one, that I guarantee (absolute words) you will have a positive experience."*

- Where might you use divorcing?
- Divorcing may also be used to divorce the service department from your company in the past, from the new mood in your service department.
- If your company has had numerous owners, you have learned this divorcing concept for your own survival, haven't you?
- That said, be very cautious never to talk about your employee or any fellow teammates.
- You can understand the feelings of your customer without agreeing with those feelings when she is attacking your company.
- It is quite different to say, *"I understand how frustrating this is for you,"* with saying, *"We are really messing up."*

DOMINANCE NEEDS (CUSTOMER)

40

Help the person with power and authority needs to see how your product fits his ideas.

"I learned so much from you in our last conversation, Mr. Carlton. I talked with my sales manager and he agrees that the industry needs a product that fits the needs you are anticipating in the future. What we do have today is a product that will work for you today. We would love you to try it and give us your advise about it's effectiveness."

A customer with dominance needs loves power and control over others. An encourager recognizes a customer's needs for dominance by the customer's power and authority needs. This person must feel as though he has made the decision because he is smarter, knows more and hates to admit somebody can offer him something. The ideas must come from him.

Dominance needs are almost instantaneously revealed in the themes under his words. *"I'm in charge of over 70 people." "They should have asked me. I've been saying that for years." "I could run this country better than the President." "I have the best business in the area."* An encourager couples the product to help fulfill this person's dominance needs.

- Its hard not to get upset with some people who have dominant needs. But lighten up. Have fun. Recognize that the underlying dynamic of a person with dominant needs is, *"Unless, I'm boss and in control, I'm worthless!"* The dominator needs, for her own temporary feeling of well being, to be in charge.
- Make your goal of selling more important that your ego's need to compete with the dominator. Ask yourself, *"Which, if any, of your products can help fulfill dominance needs?"*
- Always help the person with dominance needs realize that your product was his idea?
- Let the dominator dominate the conversation. The more she talks the more you learn. The more you learn the more you are able to draw from her ideas the reason why your product is best for her.
- Communicate your respect for the achievements of the person with domination needs.
- Remember previous conversations and proud moments of the dominating person.

41 DOOR-IN-THE-FACE" TECHNIQUE

Ask for something big, and if the customer says, 'No,' be prepared to ask for something smaller.

- Start by thinking bigger than you expect and allow the customer to use up one or two, *"No's."*
- After three *"No's"* talk about the customer's desired product qualities (See Desired Product Qualities)

Imagine the following phone call.

Caller: *"Would you be willing to give $50.00 for the local Teen Center?"*

(This may work about two or three per cent of the time.)

Now imagine this following phone call.

Caller: *"Would you be willing to donate a week of your time volunteering with local teens at the Teen Center?"*

Recipient: *"Sorry, I can't."*

Caller: *"Well, would you be willing to donate $50.00 for the local Teen Center?"*

Recipient: *"Oh, ok."*

The chances of successfully getting the contribution for the important cause doubles to triples just by using the *"Door-in-the-Face"* Technique

The *"Door-in-the-face,"* technique is a strategy for gaining a concession in which, after someone is first given an opportunity to turn down a large request (the door in the face), the same requester makes a counteroffer with a more reasonable request. Its almost as if the customer ran out of, *"no's."*

EGO VS. GOAL INFLUENCED SELLING

42

Make your selling goal more important than your ego.

The ego has a horrible way of detouring us on our journey to success in both selling and life.

As a marriage therapist, I was continually fascinated with conflicts between husbands and wives. Most disagreements do not have a goal of searching for the best answer, but rather are influenced by each person's ego's need to win the argument.

In one particular battle, the husband and wide started fighting over how many people lived in the state of Idaho. I was pleased to hear this struggle because it was a conflict that we could at least find an answer. Fortunately, I had a book that listed the 1980's census. As they are yelling at each other, I stopped the discussion with my book and reassured them that we can find the answer, and we all will be more enlightened. Interestingly, neither was particularly thrilled that we could get an answer to this issue that was obviously troubling them.

I read the 1980 census that revealed how many people lived in Idaho. I knew what was going on here. Neither the husband, nor the wife were looking for the information. Both were just looking to win, to be right, and by now, even to see the other one lose. The wife, by the way was much closer. And the hurt defensive husband asked me, *"When was that census taken!"* Both husband and wife were influenced by their egos, not their goals.

Where has your ego interfered and possibly lost a sale or a customer? What things could you have done to stay on the winning course? Perhaps taking a deep breath and listening to the customer? Maybe by giving the customer credit for her observations rather than showing her where she was wrong?

Being influenced by one's goals, and not one's ego may be part of the answer to sales motivation success. Plus being goal influenced may be the answer to life! The encourager is more interested in the goal of selling to help the customer, than in winning an argument for the sake of his ego.

- Be a credit giver, never a credit taker.
- Analyze the situation and correct it, rather than analyze who is to blame.
- Ego influenced people fight to the end to prove that they are right; goal influenced people aren't interested in who is right, but are interested in what is the best way?
- When hearing *"no"* don't interpret that as a personal rejection (ego), but rather think, *"What was the specific reason for the person's 'no?'"* (goal)
- When failing at something in life simply think, "What did I learn from this experience that will help me become better?"
- Stay focused on the goal rather than staying focused on looking good personally.
- See mistakes and rejections as opportunities to learn and correct and grow.

43 EMOTIONAL APPEALS OR LOGICAL APPEALS?

Sell excitement to the customer moved by emotion; Sell reason and logic to the customer moved by logical appeals.

- Get your customers with an emotional bias excited about your products.
- People with an emotional bias like to make decisions based on what feel's right.
- People with a belief bias are very organized and feel comfortable with you by being on time and organized.
- Don't waste this customer's time.
- Offer no fluff to the customer with a belief bias. Be soft spoken and to the point.
- Avoid emotional appeals as they turn the customer with a belief or thinking bias off.
- Belief biased people love numbers and statistics.
- Identify your customers who have an emotional, as opposed to a belief bias. While those with a belief bias you would sell with logic, reason, features and benefits, those with an emotional bias respond to an emotional appeal.

"We just met and fell in love. A month later we were married! Everybody told us we were crazy!" OR "Well, I'm sitting in my hairstylists chair and I suddenly say, 'Give me something new and wild.'" OR "I just walked into the showroom, and there was this convertible and two hours later I was driving it out!"

A customer with an emotional bias is one who is moved by feelings, emotions, the heart, and spontaneity. Emotionally motivated people want what they want, and they want it now. Like impulsive individuals, emotionally driven people make buying decision based on feelings.

"Well, we've been going out for three years now and we love each other. We want to make sure that we are ready financially and emotionally, socially, and spiritually compatible before we make the commitment to marriage."

"My hairdresser talked to me about a new style, and I told her that I would think it over and ask a few friends to see if it makes sense."

"I've been studying cars and their performances in Consumer Reports. I've made a list of advantages and disadvantages of the top three performers and plan on buying a new car next September."

Contrarily, a customer with a belief or thinking bias is moved primarily by thoughts, logic, reasoning and what makes sense. A believer or thinker uses mental charts of the advantages and disadvantages of taking certain courses of action. A believer loves planning ahead, and likes a reasonable amount of certainty before buying. She takes actions based on solid facts. A customer with a belief bias is one whose attitude is most easily modified by focusing in on changing her beliefs. The road to attitude change of a person with a belief bias is through the head, the mind, the thoughts and beliefs. The use of logic, common sense and benefits that appeal to reason are the most effective.

EMPATHY

44

Listen for the feelings under your customer's words.

While working with a real estate agent in Kentucky, my eyes were opened wide by a curious turn of events that you will now recognize as the boomerang effect. Every sales pro has gone through one of these twisters. Follow this conversation.

Customer: *"I like the house. Is this in a good school district?"*

Realtor: *"Absolutely, I think the best in the county. In fact, people buy in this area because of the schools."*

Customer: *"I'm sorry to hear that. My wife and I have no children and we are tired of paying big taxes for something we aren't going to use. That was one of the things that bugged us in Sacramento. Let's look around some more."*

Wow, I saw that one live! Who would have ever guessed that a good school district, which I learned it was, would be a deterrent?

Empathy could have avoided this whole problem. Empathy is the skill of feeling the world out of the other person's heart, seeing the world out of the other person's eyes, and hearing out of the other person's ears. Had the Realtor felt the world from the customer's perspective, he would have at least known that his customer had no children. He would have realized the school district question to be a curious one considering that fact. All in all, if the salesperson had the information on school taxes, he might have been able to show that, despite the fact that this house was in the best school district in the county, the school taxes were not higher. And, since the school district was the best, the customer's resale value would be higher to a customer who had children and would be buying from him.

Empathy makes the difference. And, in fact, empathy is considered by psychologists to be the #1 human relations skill.

Be cautious about crossing the line from empathy to sympathy. While empathy is communicating, *"I understand your anger,"* sympathy is moving in with the person's feelings and experiencing it for her, *"I am angry too."*

- There are two things we do when listening to another person: (1) We listen and judge the other from our world (apathy), or (2) We listen and understand the other person from the other person's world (empathy)
- When listening to your customer, turn her words into feelings. Ask yourself, "What might she be feeling if she said what she said?"
- Share back her feelings to her, *"Sounds like you're pretty (upset) (angry) (excited) (overwhelmed) etc."*
- Listen with empathy, rather than with sympathy. If you are too tired at the end of a day that seems that you are emotionally drained, it is often because you have crossed the line into sympathy.
- You can understand, without agreeing, with the complaining customer.

45 ENCOURAGEMENT

Understand your customer's thoughts and feelings, then center on your customer's strengths, assets and resources to build her.

- Listen for words and feelings of your customer.
- Focus on what's right with your customer.
- Recognize his strengths and assets.
- Notice efforts.
- Recognize improvements and progress.
- Believe in your customer, even more than she believes in herself.
- Lighten up, be easy to be with.
- Be goal, not ego influenced.
- Be honest.
- Help your customer to grow.

Who was the most encouraging person in your life? What qualities did he or she have? After asking thousands of people the qualities of their encourager, seven similarities surfaced. Although they explained their encourager in many different ways, these were the big seven:

1. My encourager really listened to me.
2. My encourager really understood me and how I felt (empathy).
3. My encourager saw what was right with me (asset focusing).
4. My encourager believed in me (even more than I believed in myself).
5. My encourager had a sense of humor.
6. My encourager was honest.
7. My encourager wanted what was best for me.

Winston Churchill concluded that if he could only have one quality in life, it would be courage, because if he had courage he could acquire every other quality. How do we develop courage? By definition... through encouragement.

Encouragement involves providing conditions that will most likely lead to customer courage to overcome discouraging resistances and examine new beliefs, feelings and intended actions, such as buying behaviors.

The encouraging salesman believes in his customer and in his product and encourages the customer to grab the benefits that the product has to offer.

ENTHUSIASM

46

Bring your product to life!

"No problem, we can do it!" is always Michael's response. The popular Melbourne Beach, Florida clothier can handle anything. *"If you need the suit tailored immediately, you got it."* It is never a battle getting that little extra favor from the smiling entrepreneur. No other clothing store can with the enthusiastic, *"no problem,"* demeanor of Michael.

Putting a second level on my home was exciting for me. I pictured windows that would be able to look north over the dancing Atlantic Ocean and watch the launches at Cape Kennedy. I brought in two builders. The first climbed the ladder on to the roof, moaning and groaning about his back pains. And that was just the start. For the next half hour, he blurted a litany of troubles the project will bring. *"The nails are going to cost extra because of rusting from the ocean, plus you'll have to paint this every year, the salt water is nasty, the current construction may not be strong enough to support the second floor, and it'll be big bucks to get the necessary..., etc., etc."*

You get the feeling here, that I, the customer, was feeling? And here comes John, the second builder. Walking up the latter his enthusiasm was building. *"Can't wait to see the view up here,"* he shouted as you looked down the ladder at me.

John goes to the edge of the roof, hand over his eyebrows like a visor, stares north and south and exalts, *"This is one of the finest views I have ever seen. You might want to consider all Pella Windows Oceanside, and we can add a fireplace over here riverside. This is going to be fun. If I cut a little off the cost, will you invite me over here for your first party?"* And he laughs.

Which of the two builders do you want to be living with, every day for about two months while the second story is being built? John got the job and did the work beautifully, and yes, I still had to pay for the special nails, etc. but that's OK.

Enthusiasm made the difference.

- Be quick to spot opportunities for enthusiasm.
- Smile enthusiastically.
- Walk enthusiastically.
- Speak enthusiastically.
- Use enthusiastic words. Things aren't just OK. Things are terrific!
- Answer your phone enthusiastically.
- Bring your product to life.
- Plant dreams in your customer's mind.
- Arouse your customer's feelings.
- Get enthused about the small details.
- Remember those stress relieving words, *"No problem!"*

47 EXHIBITION NEEDS

Show how your product will help the customer with exhibition needs to be noticed.

- What behaviors might you observe in a person with exhibition needs?
- Which of your products will appeal to the customer with exhibition needs?
- Words like, *"New!" "Flashy!" "Latest!" "Hot!"*
- Be enthused about your customer with exhibition needs. They love it!
- Communicate, *"You're the one I've been waiting for."*
- Ask, *"what's new?"* and you have a new story that goes on and on for hours.
- Let this person know there is no one like him. He is unique.
- Don't bore this customer, be prepared and keep your presentation moving.

Paris Hilton. How would you sell her your product? How would you approach Jim Carrey? Or Richard Simmons? What would be an interesting way of making a sales presentation to Robin Williams? That may be impossible!

You probably wouldn't want to bore any of these three customers. My guess is that you would come to life, wearing bells and whistles and bringing out your enthusiastic best. That's the mode to be in when you are selling a person with exhibition needs.

People with exhibition needs are the life of the party, or of your business. They are creative. They are quick with a joke or a song. And they don't have the problem of being too inhibited. Their fashion is exciting, stimulating and edgy. They have the courage to spontaneously express themselves and they dare go where others just watch. Never call people with exhibition needs boring.

Customers with exhibition needs have a desire to be seen, to show off and be the center of attention. An encourager quickly recognizes the customer with exhibition needs and sells the product to fulfill those exhibition needs, whenever possible.

EXTINGUISHING

48

Eliminate your habits and behaviors that may turn customers off.

Learn to hear things the first time they are said. Years ago, a very polite and soft-spoken women in Lafayette, Louisiana approached me by the podium after my talk.

"Dr. Lew, I sure enjoyed your talk. If I may offer one suggestion, I was a little, uh, scared when you jumped out onto the stage at the beginning of your talk. I missed a little bit of the early part of your message because I was backing off. I thought you were a little too aggressive. But that's probably just me."

I thanked the kind lady for her help and told myself I would start off slower. About a year later, a woman in Columbus, Ohio presented the same complaint, but wasn't as soft in her criticism. I flashed back and recalled the fact that I had been told this once before. I needed two times to eliminate or extinguish my turn-off behaviors. Make a commitment to hear things the first time your customer tells you.

Extinguishing involves consciously eliminating specific behaviors that do not produce positive results.

- Cut out ineffective behaviors. If a customer coughs when you are smoking a cigarette, extinguish the cigarette figuratively and literally.
- Mack a list of complaints you heard in your past. As you look over the list, ask yourself if the criticisms were accurate or not. Then ask if these are habits or behaviors that you could give up. Make a commitment to extinguishing those behaviors that turn people off.
- Make a list of habits you need to break for your own sales effectiveness, even if no one has ever commented.
- Drink less coffee, because you are burned-out to early in the day? You can do it!
- Too much at lunch or the wrong foods at lunch which make you tired? Make the little sacrifice to get big results.
- And learn to hear things the first time they are said.

49 EYE CONTACT

Develop your confidence to look your customers in the eyes with your big smile.

- Develop your confidence and skills in looking people in their eyes.
- Let your honest emotions flow that reflect your customer's feelings.
- Be like Tom Gude. Imagine experiencing your customer's success through your eyes.
- Experience your customer's hurt and rejection through your through your eyes.
- Create sparkling eyes.
- Create wide-eyed surprise through your eye communication.
- Sense the positioning and range of your eyelids.

We can speak or communicate that we are listening through our eyes. Our eyes can also reflect the feelings of the customer's words.

One salesperson with whom I travel in Iowa is particularly genuine in his eye contact. When Tom Gude listens to one of his customers reveal a very difficult experience, Tom's eyes moisten up because he really feels it. Tom is there with her. When another client tells Tom she is now a grandmother for the first time, his eyes sparkle with joy for her. I also saw surprise in his eyes when another customer gave him a gift. And all of this happened in one day!

Effective salespersons have the ability to use an ideal amount of eye contact. What is ideal? Obviously, too little or no eye contact might be perceived as disinterest or lack of confidence. On the other hand, constant staring may be threatening and produce defensiveness in the client. The ideal amount of eye contact is one in which the sales person feels comfortable, with a few breaks in contact.

Another function of contact is to convey empathy for the other person's concerns. Often when the salesperson interrupts the customer who is speaking, the customer loses her train of thought. By communicating through one's eyes that he is in touch, the salesperson can encourage the customer to continue speaking with someone who is truly listening.

Eye contact involves looking directly into the other person's eyes. An encourager uses eye contact to communicate authority, confidence in the message, genuineness and congruence.

50

FACTUAL RESISTANCES

Stay with the facts with person whose resistance is based on facts, not emotions.

"No, I don't want to use your credit card because of its extremely high interest rates."

"I am not interested in this vacuum cleaner. The manufacturer didn't support me when I had problems with the last model."

"I need a bigger house for this same price."

Whenever someone doesn't buy and knows exactly and specifically why, the salesperson is hearing a factual resistance. Factual resistances are occurring when the customer doesn't buy because of certain facts about the product or cost. The encourager addresses the factual resistance in the spirit that, *"I must show this person more factual benefits of buying. If I truly believe I can't, or that this customer has a better product for her at this moment, I will acknowledge her wise choice."*

- Connect to your customer's way of thinking. *"Why pay more than you have to?"*
- Remember empathy and turn the customers words into feelings, *"Sounds like you're pretty frustrated that..."*
- When the resistance is factual, stay with the facts, and add additional facts that the customer is missing.
- Use numbers and facts, than facts, then numbers.
- The great news for you about hearing a factual resistance is that you have the meat of the objection to deal with. The devil you know!
- Take the objection, for example, the high credit card interest rate and respond, *"So, if I can get lower interest rates for you, would you then be interested?"*

51 FINANCIAL MOTIVATION NEEDS (CUSTOMER)

- What are some questions you hear from a person who has financial motivation needs?
- Everything boils down to cost to the financially motivated person. Price out your product by the ounce, or by smaller quantities.
- Emphasize any savings in buying in big bulk.
- Highlight specials!
- Never forget to talk up the word "sale," pointing out how much is saved in real dollars, and in percentages.
- Make comparisons whenever possible with other products while giving a benefit that your product has that the other doesn't.
- If your product has high concentration in its usage, point out that the customer will use less, making it less costly.
- Start and finish your presentation with the words, "Here's the bottom line!"

Sell bottom line people the long term bottom line.

The comedian Jack Benny's character was one driven by financial needs motivation. Someone once joked of Benny that a thief pulled out a gun at Benny and demanded, *"Your money or your life."* When Benny didn't respond immediately, the nervous thief repeated his demand, *"OK, which one, your money or your life?"* And Benny, with his index finger and thumb to his chin finally responded, *"I'm thinking!"*

The financially motivated person is like most of us. But, here we are talking about a customer who is far out in his concern for cost. Realtors call him a *"low baller."* He's the "bottom line guy." He still remembers what he *"used to pay for this product."* Easy to understand. And hard to sell if the salesperson doesn't have the lowest price.

A person with financial motivational needs is driven by money. The person with financial motivation needs quickly gets into the issue of cost. The encourager has to be creative to demonstrate the long term benefits of the encourager's product with an emphasis on cost.

"FOOT-IN-THE-DOOR" APPROACH

52

Get a small commitment before asking for the big commitment from your customer.

I met very few people who would walk up to a person they were attracted to but never met before, and ask the person, "*Will you marry me?*" And of the few people I met who would pop the early question, none succeeded. There are just too many steps along the way in between "*nice to meet you,*" and "*I do!*" One first has to get her, "*foot-in-the-door.*"

The effectiveness of the foot-in-the-door approach was first discovered by psychologists Jonathan Freedman and Scott Fraser. They reported that a researcher, posing as a volunteer worker asked for something ridiculous from random homeowners. The researchers inquired if the house owners would allow a billboard to be placed on their lawn reading, "*Drive Safely*!" Of course only a few would agree to such a intrusive request.

However, read this, a full 76% agreed to do so if – if they previously accepted and displayed the volunteer worker's three inch square sign to be a "*Be a Safe Driver.*"

The "*foot-in-the-door*" approach involves encouraging the customer to make a small commitment first, before asking for a bigger commitment. This is the opposite of the "*door-in-the-face*" technique which asks for something big first to accept something smaller. An example of the "*foot-in-the-door,*" approach is simply asking someone if he would consider trying one product- to get the foot in the door- and start building the relationship and demonstrating great service.

- How could you make use of the "*foot-in-the-door*" technique in your work?
- What is the smallest possible request you could ask for just to get your foot in the door?
- Develop a hierarchy of requests beginning with your smallest to your largest.
- You will soon learn the "*go for the gold approach*" where you dream of what your ultimate success day would be like? Tie "*go for the gold*" in with the "*foot-in-the-door*" technique.
- Be prepared to start at the highest request that has a reasonable amount of certainty of success.

53 FOREWARNING

Demonstrate your confidence that a product is so right for your customer that you tell her you are going to sell her.

- In what circumstances could you employ forewarning?
- Apply forewarning cautiously and in those instances that you have a 90% certainty your customer will buy.
- Do your homework up front. When you see a product come out that you know a customer will love, call on them, and forewarn them.
- Always smile enthusiastically when using forewarning.

Forewarning involves telling a customer with whom you feel comfortable that you are warning him, ahead of time, that you are about to sell him. Forewarning is for the gutsy, confident salesperson with a sense of humor, who has built a great relationship with a customer.

Susan, a Pennsylvania sales consultant gave her customers as much time as they needed. You could say she was accessible. She knew every customer, and every one of their children's names, and birthdays! And she was one of the best I've ever seen. When I traveled with Susan, she would tell me, at the beginning of the day which customer will buy which product. She cut out time by using forewarning, and her customers appreciated the time Susan saved them.

Forewarning involves telling the customer with whom you feel comfortable that you are going to persuade him to take action. Forewarning reveals your absolute confidence and belief in this product for this person.

Forewarning is most effective when four conditions are present: (1) you have a great relationship with this customer, (2) you have a passion for a particular product, (3) you know the product fits your customer's product needs, and (4) you are convinced the product fits your customer's personality needs. If all four of these conditions are present, forewarning will be a success.

GO FOR THE GOLD

54

Go for the biggest realistic goal possible, make a plan, and go for it

Dennis, the publisher of this book, and I met with this big corporation. We had the goal of coupling one of my earlier books with the company's newest product. The company had a new product line coming out and I thought the book would be a perfect compliment to attract customers to buy it. I thought maybe the marketing people would be interested in a thousand or so copies. Dennis thought differently.

Five minutes into the meeting Dennis heard that the company had 16,000 regular customers in a special club they had created.

"Sounds to me like 16,000 books would be your first order. What a great gift this book would be to add value to your product," Dennis concluded.

"Great idea, what do you other guys think?" asked the VP of marketing. All agreed.

And then Dennis put the customizing finish on the sale. *"How about if we design the book cover exactly to resemble your product label?"*

Done deal. Twenty minutes, 16,000 books sold. I would have been thrilled with 2,000. But Dennis is a big thinker who decided to go for the gold.

- What would you consider to be a huge day of sales for you?
- Imagine if you planned for one day in the next two weeks to have that big day.
- What would the most logical day be for you?
- How could you achieve your big daydream?
- Make your plan.
- Go for the Gold!

55 "GOT IT MOMENT"

*The "**Got It Moment**" happens when the encourager's message connects with the customer. In this moment the encourager moves rapidly to close the sale*

- What clues do you observe in the customer at the *"Got It Moment?"*
- Become an expert in sensing the *"I got it moment"*
- Let the customer who just had the *"got it moment"* talk.
- Nod your head, smile and feel the customer's enthusiasm.
- If it feels right say to the customer, *"You got it!"*
- Avoid overkill and save your customer's time after he experiences the *"I got it moment."*
- Close the sale using your customer's words.

Every sales person knows that energizing moment in selling. The customer's head starts nodding, the smile grows wider, the arms come up, and the customer wants to speak. She's got it! Picture some images in your mind.

A teacher is explaining geometry to her struggling student in a way that it finally hits him. Sense the teen's reaction. Perhaps he looks up and responds, *"Ohhhh! I got it!!!"* His eyes open wider, he smiles, and he is now wiser than he was a moment ago.

This is the, *"I got it moment!"* The *"I got it moment"* is the goal of not only educating, it is the goal of selling. After all, selling is advancing people through education and encouragement.

56

IMPROVEMENT NOTICING

Spot progress in your customer, especially when it is your product that is helping.

The French father of autosuggestion Emile Coue' advised us to tell ourselves, *"Each and every day, I'm getting better and better in every way!"*

Heidi brought her spelling test into her guidance counselor's office every Friday. For the first half of the year she had ten for ten wrong in her spelling. Finally in early January she showed up at the counselor's door discouraged and said, *"I got nine wrong in spelling."*

Her encouraging counselor quickly came over to the little girl and enthusiastically responded, *"Wow, Heidi, you spelled the word 'cat' correctly. Look at how you are improving. Did you know that nobody in the whole wide world can spell the word cat better than you?"*

Heidi thought and replied, *"Nobody?"*

"That's right, Heidi, even though there are a lot of people who will tie you, nobody does it better."

Like the school counselor, the encourager notices improvement to show the customer that what he bought has really improved his life, filled his needs or solved his problems.

- Think of your customer in a *"Before and After"* picture. Remind him of where he was before and how far he has come (hopefully through your product, but notice anyway).
- Make a phone call now to a past customer and communicate your improvement noticing. Listen for her surprised tone.
- Acknowledgement that dress she is wearing that she bought from you, or the car she drove up in if she purchased it from your dealership.
- Notice efforts that your customer is making. *"I see you are really working hard.... Keep up the good work. You know that I'm here for you."* (accessibility)
- Encourage your customer, *"Keep progressing, you'll soon be there."*
- Speak in the language of improvement, *"Look at the progress you are making,"* or *"You may feel you have not reached your goal yet, but look how far you have come."*
- Think improvement, effort, progress, and growth.

57 INDIVIDUATION NEEDS (CUSTOMER)

Make notes of customers who see themselves as individuals and who don't buy a popular product especially because everyone else does.

Jerry Garcia of *The Grateful Dead* fame claimed that he didn't want to be the best of the best. He wanted to be seen as doling something different. It has been suggested that Kurt Cobain of *Nirvana* committed suicide because his music became popular, and was welcomed into mainstream. He was counterculture.

You can predict my friend Jon's decision on buying any product. If everyone else, or anyone else likes it, he doesn't! While some are trying to keep up with the Jones, Jon will not buy anything that the Jones' buy. Jon has a strong need to be different. The non-conformist, in fact, may not buy the best product, or the least expensive product. He buys the product that no one else has. Jon is moved by individuation needs.

Most salespersons, playing the averages, miss the opportunity to sell Jon. That is understandable, but why not increase one's sales potential by always being aware that the customer in front of me now could be one like Jon. Individuation needs are in operation when a person resists buying or resists a trend because of a desire to be different. People with individuation needs have a strong striving for uniqueness, and are in a sense saying, *"Don't judge me by the popular standard. I'm not like them. I'm special, different and have a mind of my own. If you notice that I'm unique, you'll have a sale."*

- Who isn't buying your most popular product because everyone has it? This is a clue as to how to effectively meet this person's needs for being different. Sell them on a product that is different, that very few people have.
- Spot your customer's dress, accessories, hairstyle and language to sense if this person's needs run counterculture.
- Be aware of the back off response of your customer when you use such words as *"popular."*
- Use the words, *"different," "unique," "rare,"* or *"unusual"* with the person who has individuation needs.
- If you sell only one product, vary the color for the person with individuation needs. *"Almost everyone wants blue or white. No one has bought a black one yet."*

INFORMATION SHORT CUTTING

58

Summarize all of the research, data, sales brochures, etc. into a crisp, brief message that gets to the point

The public support for the complex air traffic control strike of 1982 was brought to an abrupt halt by a sentence from President Ronald Reagan. As the former actor held up the contract that all of the air traffic workers signed as an agreement to be hired, Reagan pointed out that they agreed not to strike. Nothing more needed to be said. They violated their own agreement of employment. Who could support them? Reagan was a genius at information short cutting.

The elderly woman, usually a Wendy's restaurant customer tries a competitor's burger and responds with an angry, *"Where's the beef?"* The little diapered tike sits on a Michelin tire and the commercial reminds the viewer, *"there's a lot riding on your tire!"* Short. To the point. Effective. No graphs or charts or statistics involved with this point. Just a phrase that sums it all up.

Information short cutting involves breaking down massive information into a catchy phrase that is digestible and crisply clarifies the benefits while connecting to the customer's needs.

You can learn quickly about information short cutting by listening to 15-30 second commercials on the radio or watching them on TV. There it is, the whole story in 15 seconds.

- Which product has too long of a story that loses your customer's attention?
- Gather all of the data and information you have on your product. Develop two versions, the long one for your customers with a logical bias, and the information short cut version for your busy, or impulsive customers with an emotional bias
- Identify pulse point, such as benefits, cost, quality, value, etc.
- Develop catchy phrases that summarize your product's benefits. They will get to the point while respecting your customer's time
- Tell your customer, *"I could go on and on about this product if you like, but I sense that your time is precious, so let me get right to it."*
- Repeat the short cut information frequently.

59 INNER DIRECTED OR OUTER DIRECTED BUYER?

Allow the inner directed buyer to draw her own conclusion. Draw the conclusion for the outer directed buyer.

In my stint as both a waiter, and short order cook at my mother's restaurant, about one out of every seven or eight customers would ask me (the perceived expert), "What do you recommend?" or "What looks good today?" My deepest thoughts, which I didn't share, were that the cheeseburger looked better than the hamburger. But I usually upgraded the inquiring customer into the higher, more metaphysically evolved level, "*Salisbury Steak.*" More often than not, the customer complied. I learned later that these counter customers were "*outer-directed buyers.*" The outer-directed customer prefers that the salesperson make the decision. After all the salesperson is the expert, isn't he?

Other customers knew what they wanted. If I only had one filled cabbage left and a pile of stuffed peppers, I would hope they would choose the stuffed peppers but no amount of tilting the sale another way would shift the inner-directed customer's decision. These customers made the decision from within. They were inner-directed buyers.

An inner directed consumer makes decisions based upon her own (inner) conclusions and often has a psychological reactance (boomerang effect) to someone else drawing her conclusion. The encourager presents the case and then allows the inner directed person to draw her own conclusions.

- Become a scientist of understanding customer motivation. Tune in quickly to determine if a customer is inner or outer directed as a buyer
- One of the first observations to make when meeting a customer is to determine if this person is inner (what makes sense or gives a good feeling to me) or outer directed (tell me what to do, what is everybody having, etc.)
- Allow the inner directed person to make her own decision.
- Guide the outer directed person directly to the conclusion.
- Be cautious about the dangers of drawing the conclusion for the outer directed buyer. Those who are passively resistive may want you to take responsibility so that they can point out to you that it was your fault that the order was wrong or bad, and they deserve a refund.

INOCULATION

60

Prompt your customer, up front, to see through your competitor's message.

Yogi Berra may or may not have said, "You can hear a lot by listening." There's a lot of truth to that. At a recent neighborhood party, I introduced Carl, who owns a successful local appliance store to another neighbor, Dorothy, a recent arrival to the outer circle. Imagine yourself standing near, sipping your Merlot, and listening to the following conversation. (I will attempt to construct these words in the best possible light to make my point on inoculation).

Dorothy: *"Lew tells me that your family owns a local store where I can buy a dishwasher and dryer. I apologize but I've never heard of you. I hear constant commercials on the radio from another appliance store. Coincidentally, I was going to go there next week."*

Carl: *"I understand Dorothy. Our competitor has some great and funny commercials. They are always on the local radio. My family and I talked it over. We decided that instead of spending our money on advertising, we would pass that savings on to our customers. It's just a business decision. If people price both places, on the same product, they'll see our advantage to them."*

Dorothy: *"Hmm, sounds like the customer is paying for your competitor's advertising."*

Carl: *"Yeah, each time you hear the commercial, just think to yourself, 'I wonder which customer bought that radio time?'" (inoculation)*

With Dorothy's help, Carl inoculated her to experience a backfiring of the competitor's message. The more messages, the more turned off she was to Carl's competitor. Through the brilliance of inoculation. Inoculation happens when the encourager provides the customer with an argument, up front and before, the customer will hear a presentation from a competitor. If you know the benefits your competitor will highlight, inoculate your customer to be wary of such sales pitches. Give a refute to the competitor's argument.

- When inoculating suggest, "If ever you hear someone tell you that their product does this or that, immediately say to yourself,…." (inoculation)
- Encourage your customer to *"think" "hear" "see" "experience"* the words of the message in a new way.
- The more your competitor delivers the message, the more ineffective the message.
- Carl and Dorothy are not the real names, but if either picks this book up, I think he or she will figure it out.

61 "KERNEL OF TRUTH" EXPOSURE

When hearing an objection based on true but limited information, encourage the customer to see the full picture.

"If it doesn't fit, you must acquit!" attorney Johnny Cochran confidently told the jury of the O .J. Simpson trial. At first glance, and at first hearing, the thought does make sense, and sound right. I mean, it even rhymes. It must be true. But just because something is partially true doesn't mean it is totally true. Just because the glove doesn't fit does not mean that Simpson was not guilty, does it?

A person is a victim of the kernel of truth when the person hears part of the story, and then concludes that the whole story is true. In selling, the salesperson is up against the kernel of truth when a customer offers a resistance based on some belief she has that is only partially true. The encourager combats the kernel of truth by asking questions that expose the error of generalizing.

Automobile Salesman: *"So you go shopping on your scooter? Why?"*

Customer: *"Because it never broke down."*

Automobile Salesman: *"Well, that's true, I'll bet. How long does it take for you to get there, and how inconvenient is it to carry those packages, and how cold is it, etc. I'd like to suggest a better way. A car that will save you valuable time, is warmer, and won't brake down!"*

Of course the example is absurd, but when you hear a kernel of truth, think of that scooter.

- When you hear a benefit of a competitor's line from a customer, respond, "Yes, there is a kernel of truth to that. I believe that part is correct. But you want to know the bigger picture before you buy, don't you?"
- My attorney neighbor, after hearing the other side present their case, and offer its kernel of truth, brushes his hands together and tells the jury, "You've heard the view of my colleague who presented a shrewdly selected part of the facts. But now let me fill out the full picture. Here is, 'the rest of the story!'" (exposing the kernel of truth, all the while piggy backing on years of Paul Harvey's credibility.)
- While our competitor is offering you a TV, what we have here is a Home Entertainment Center.
- While the elephant's ear is the elephant's ear, the elephant's ear is not the whole elephant.
- *"I agree that your current product does have this benefit. You value that. I'd like to show you to a product that has not only that benefit that you need, but a few other benefits, as well. Are you interested?"*

KEY WORDS

62

Identify 3 key words before each presentation, and repeat each word about 5 times.

"Cold Drinks," old Runt Runyon would bellow out at the Municipal Memorial Stadium under the hot summer baseball sky. That was 40 years ago and I still remember those words and that rugged, purposeful voice. You knew why Runt was there, what he was selling, and when you saw him downtown on another day, you had a craving for a Royal Crown Cola. *"Cold Drinks"* were his key words.

"Lowest Price Anywhere"

"The Freshest Seafood on Earth. Your Meal Slept in The Bay Last Night"

"Guaranteed...For Your Lifetime!"

The key words are the ones the encouraging salesperson repeats to the customer throughout the presentation. Key words shout to the customer, *"This is what this product is all about!"* Key words are sharp, crisp, well defined, clear, no shade of gray, streamlined, no messing around. Key words cut right to needs and, while ruling out some, pull in others.

Sometimes customers reveal benefits that are important to them through their words. Listen carefully to use your customer's own words as your key words.

- Choose three key words for each of your products.
- Product A, key words:
- Product B, key words:
- Product C, key words:
- Repeat these key words throughout the presentation.
- Be open to include new key words that your customer starts using when talking about your product.
- Let me repeat: Use your customer's key words.

63 MATCHING

Get your behavior cues directly from your customer's behaviors.

- Match as many aspects of your customer's behavior as possible.
- The faster your customer speaks, the faster you speak.
- Match your rhythm with the customer's rhythm.
- Match your words with your customer's words.
- Match your body language with your customer's body language.
- The more expressive your customers are, the more animated you become.
- Flexibility is the key in encouragement selling.
- Adapt yourself to your customer. Get your behavior cues from your customer's behaviors.

A great way of mastering the skill of matching is to imagine that you are selling Seinfeld's "soft talker." Do you remember, "the soft talker?" She was quiet and very difficult to understand. Picture people who you know in your life who are so timid and so light with their voice that you have to ask them a few times to repeat what they said. How do you approach the timid person in your presentation?

The skilled salesperson's presentation is dramatically different to the soft talker than it is in selling the boisterous Kramer. Remember Kramer? His arms flew like Holland windmills, and his aggressive voice backed people off. How do you sell Kramer?

Same product, yet two different presentation styles.

What is the answer? Simple. You get your selling cues by matching each person's behavior.

An effective presentation to the soft talker is a soft, slow style. Arms down, head lowered, calm facial expression, and extremely patient.

Now selling Kramer, that's a different story. Let those arms fly, bring out the range of facial expressions, and speak fast.

In fact, customers who speak fast want to pull the words out of the mouth of the slow talking salesperson. And customers who are slow talkers may be intimidated by the fast talking salesperson.

Matching is adopting your customer's body language, facial gestures, speed of speech, and words to get your self into a rhythmic rapport with her. Let your customer's behaviors be the cues for your behaviors.

MAXIMINI SELLING

64

Create a list maximizing the benefits, and minimizing the risk of your products.

My cousin Larry can sell anybody anything without breaking a sweat. He is the ultimate influenologist. In his usual soft spoken manner, the intellectual adjusts his glasses when he makes a point suggesting that his customer do the same and look more clearly at the selling contract. He'll push the contract over to you so that you can see every detail. Larry has nothing to hide. And then Larry presents a bullet by bullet point outlining first, the minimum risks, followed by maximizing the five to ten benefits of buying.

And you are happy you bought, thrilled that he gave you the time. You are reassured that you will soon hear if your mortgage went through. And I have bought more than one mortgage through Larry. I not only appreciate his style, but chances are I wouldn't have the home I do without Larry's encouragement and help to see that I can do it.

Maximini selling involves maximizing the benefits and minimizing the risk.

- Know up front how you will maximini sell each product to each customer need.
- Maximini selling closing involves being prepared to summarize all of the massive benefits and the minimal risks of the product immediately before asking for the sale.
- Be prepared for hitting that grand slam in the bottom of the ninth.
- Tell the customer, *"Remember these 3 points."* And list them: *"1 - 2 – 3."*
- Use maximini selling, like Larry does, at the point of closing.

65 MIRRORING

Mirror the body language and facial expressions of your customer to help her sense synchronically.

- Practice mirroring in your everyday conversations with people.
- When mirroring a total stranger it is not uncommon for the person to ask you, *"Don't I know you from somewhere?"*

The brilliant psychiatrist Milton Erikson was so effective with people that he was taped and studied by others. Why was this therapist so influential? Amazing as it seems, Dr. Erikson's body language was part of the clue to his influence on people. He consciously, or non-consciously mirrored his patients' behaviors.

Mirroring is adapting your customer's behaviors, but in a way it looks like the customer is looking into a mirror at himself. If one pictures herself looking into a mirror at herself she will notice that when she moves her left hand on her body, it appears that the right hand is moving in the mirror.

For example, mirroring involves moving one's left hand when the mirror image moves their right hand when facing each other. Psychological studies have revealed that those who are most effective with others consciously or non-consciously mirror the others behavior.

NOVELTY NEEDS (CUSTOMER)

66

Sell people with novelty needs something exciting, gimmicky, a change. "I must have it now!" "How much?"

The person with novelty needs has an interesting home filled with everything that one day sparkled and shined, but now is on the backburner because new things have arrived to take their place. Hula hoops now too small, dog collars with no dogs are no longer being walked and new gimmicks take the spotlight. The salesperson's job is customer satisfaction, and the person with novelty needs has every right to be as satisfied as any other customer.

A customer with novelty needs is stimulated by change, breaks from the routine, gimmicks or anything different. The word "*new*" is a hot word for those with novelty needs. Sell the person, today, now.

- Spot the flashy customers you have with novelty needs. The ones with things hanging from their rear view mirrors.
- *"We just got these in today!"*
- Sell the car, suit or dress by selling the flashy accessories.
- Sell the cocktail by selling the yellow umbrella.
- Sell the dog by selling the dog sweater.

67 ONE-SIDED OR TWO-SIDED COMMUNICATION?

- If your customer doesn't have much time, is loyal to you and doesn't know or care about the other side, present just your side.
- If your customer originally disagrees with you and already knows the other side, present your awareness of the other view.
- If you customer will soon learn about the other side, present the other side, and then inoculate.

When do you, and don't you, present your competitor's products positive features?

Introducing a new product with a new company is an uphill trip when the competitor has a foothold on the market. Where does the salesperson begin when looking into the eyes of customers who are loyal to the dominant force in the market?

Begin by acknowledging some of the positive features and benefits of the competitor's brand. Since the customer already knows the benefits of the competitor's brand, there is little risk. Plus the sales person not only communicates a complete awareness, and more importantly, a fairness in looking at the world from the customers' perspective. In addition the sales person is communicating a respect for the customers' previous buying choices. Why would anyone want to offend a customer's previous decisions?

After communicating that the sales person is well aware of, and respects the competitor, the new product she is offering today goes well beyond the competitors in a few important ways. Because the sales professional is presenting both sides of the story, to those who already know the other side, this is known as two-sided communication.

Now, what if the sales person is working for the dominant leader in the marketplace speaking to loyal customers? Should she present one or both sides? In this instance one-sided communication is more effective because it will reinforce the beliefs already held by the loyal supportive customer.

One-sided communications are those that contain only one side, the encourager's side, to influence a customer. If however the customer is already aware or will soon learn about the competitor's benefits, two-sided communications are more effective.

OPTIMISM

68

Optimism is a state in which an encourager believes that the problems in front of them have solutions.

Optimism is a vital ingredient in encouragement selling.

In the movie *Dumb and Dumber*, Dumber asks this hot lady what his chances are with her. After being pushed for an answer she responds with the unreachable possibility of, *"A million to one!"* Dumber views this newfound hope as the breakthrough he needed by jumping for joy shouting, *"Yes!"* That's optimism!

My colleague and I walked outside on a cloudy day when he commented, *"The sun isn't out today."* I looked at him and responded, *"What?"* He looked up and insisted, *"The sun isn't out."* I stopped and asked him, *"Do you think the sun isn't out just because you can't see it? Where did the center of the universe go? The sun is always out. You just have to look beyond the clouds!"*

The optimistic salesperson faces the same daily challenges that the pessimistic salesperson faces. But the optimist has an advantage. He faces the challenges with the conviction that problems have solutions.

When you think of it, every great achievement was accomplished by an optimist. The placing of the flag on the moon, the curing of diseases, the building of businesses, and the greatest sales professionals all proceeded as if the challenges in front of them had solutions. How many streets in your town are named after pessimists, anyway? Have you ever been to a testimonial dinner for a nit picker? Have you ever seen a newspaper classified add such as, *"Looking for sales people who don't believe they can do?"*

Wake up tomorrow with the belief that your problems have answers. That belief will give you additional strength to go forward.

- The only way to go forward is to assume every sale.
- Operate out of the idea that the product you have is important, and your customer can benefit from your product.
- Proceed today as if every problem you face has a solution somewhere in the vast realm of your alive, creative mind.
- When facing a problem, or a challenge, quickly shift into the optimistic mood and look up.

69 PASSIVE RESISTANCE OR ACTIVE RESISTANCE?

Classify your customer's objections as being fake or real.

"Why did I have this gnawing feeling in my guts?" the seasoned salesman wondered. *"I mean, she was smiling, she seemed to be interested in my product, and she didn't leave."*

"How was she responding when you started to close the sale?" I inquired.

"Well, again she smiled, nodded, and would answer, 'Yes, but!'"

"Yes, but, what?"

"I don't know, it wasn't exactly clear."

"Did she buy?"

"No, she was going to think about it and get back to me."

Passive resistance is occurring when the customer appears to be interested, but neither buys, nor will directly voice her resistance. The passive resister will 'call you.'

What makes passive resisters tick? We all are passive resistant when we find ourselves in situations with someone who has authority, like our boss, or someone who is strong or dominant and we afraid to be honest. These are situations in which we may say, *"yes"* when we really mean, *"no."* Then after saying yes, we put all kinds of roadblocks up, like procrastination, pouting, getting sick, and being late. All because we can't be direct, we become passively resistant. It is almost as if we are not buying, but are not responsible for not buying. We'd like to buy, but this one thing or another is holding us back.

Contrarily, the active resistor tells you right out front why he isn't buying. With the active resister, you can grab hold of the objection and deal with the resistance directly. Its on the table.

- You are with a passive resister when you hear constant, "Yes, buts."
- When you are experiencing first, anger followed by guilt, you are with a passive resister.
- You feel it in your guts, but can't explain why you are with a passive resister.
- Your goal is to get the passive resister to be honest, specific and responsible.
- Encourage the passive resister to speak, repeat her words, listen closely, smile and encourage her to make a small commitment.
- Pin the passive resister down to details, including time, place, date, specific costs, have checks, etc.
- Expect her to be sick at closing. I've seen a saleswoman joke with her customer up front, *"Don't you be sick on Thursday for closing. OK!"*
- With the active resister, just find the resistance and deal with it directly.
- And be cautious to watch out for moments when you yourself are becoming passively resistant!

70

PERCEPTUAL ALTERNATIVES (COULD-BE-NESS THINKER)

Creatively show your customer all of the benefits of your product.

When our daughter Gabrielle was seven, she told me that she had just tried an experiment. *"I closed my eyes in my face to see if I could still see anything. And dad, when I closed my eyes in my face, I found eyes in my head. And my eyes in my head could see two birds in a tree in Alabama. Then I opened up my eyes in my face, and I couldn't see the birdies anymore. I could only see what was in my room."*

Then she thought and concluded, *"The eyes in your head can see further than the eyes in your face."*

Are you looking at the world through the eyes in your face, or through the eyes in your head?

Perceptual alternatives are the many, unlimited different ways a customer can be encouraged to look at, feel, think about or perceive a situation or a product. For example, an *"M"* could be a *"W"* or an *"E"* based upon how the person is looking at the symbol. The more perceptual alternative a customer and encourager have, the richer their benefits will be.

- Look at a pencil. The dictionary defines a pencil as a *"rod shaped object filled with graphite or lead and used for writing."* How much is that pencil worth if we take that narrow view of it? A dime or a quarter?
- Now become a could-be-ness thinker. Begin to see what that same pencil could-be. (1) It could be used to teach a class of pre-school children the color yellow, (2) it could be used to scratch your back, (3) it could be used to protect yourself if attacked, (4) it could be used to keep score on the golf course or (5) write a love letter or song, or (6) it could be used to change the course of human history. If you are selling that pencil now, that same ten-cent pencil, how much worth have you added to it by becoming a could-be-ness thinker?
- Develop your perceptual alternatives. Pick an object around you. Any object. Let your mind go crazy. No answer is wrong. Take five minutes and develop as many perceptual alternatives you can. What are all of the possible ways you can look at or think about this object. Each perceptual alternative you develop adds value to the object.
- Choose one of your products. Expand its value in the next five minutes by developing perceptual alternatives of your product. Let your mind go and flow. Jot down every thought. No answer is wrong.
- Look at your list and expand on those ideas that you consider to be the most useful
- Stop looking at the world through the eyes in your face; get a new vantage point from the eyes in your mind.
- Start increasing the value of everything around you by becoming a could-be-ness thinker.
- Remember, whatever something could-be is what the thing really is. It just needs you to bring it to life.

71 PERSISTANCE

You never fail. You just learn. And the more you learn the more successful you become.

- President Lincoln won very few elections in his life. Lincoln's persistence helped him win the Presidential Election of 1860.
- Go after the toughest account you can find and be persistent.
- Never stop believing.
- Never give up.
- Persist. Against all odds. Especially against all odds.
- Every time you look at a bottle of Biolage' shampoo remind yourself of the importance of persistence.

He told me, *"We are going to be the biggest, but more importantly the best company in the world someday. We are going to fight to have the world see that hairstyling is one of the most important professions."*

His name was Arnie Miller and he was a hairdresser who believed in his profession. He asked me to join the company and work with his team, his distributors sales forces and store people and speak to hairdressers about their important influence on peoples' lives. Arnie faced setback after setback from high interest rates to tough competition to health problems. With the support of his wife Sydell, and family, he went into the unknown knowing his mission for elevating the hairdressing profession was the only thing that mattered. The Einstein looking genius was loved by every pride filled hairdresser in the United States and Canada. And in nine years, by 1989, Arnie's company Matrix became the North American leader in only 9 years. You probably use Biolage or Amplify products today. Arnie never stopped believing and never gave up. He persisted in selling his dream!

She has a busy Japanese restaurant in Melbourne, Florida. Her ginger sauce in the best salad dressing I've ever had anywhere. Everyone told her this is a winner. Because it lacked preservatives it couldn't realistically be shipped. She ran into barrier after barrier in promoting her product beyond Brevard County. Today, you'll see Makoto's Ginger dressing in the refrigerated area of your local supermarket. One person, now with two restaurants in Melbourne Florida supplies America with Makotos. The best. She never stopped believing. She never gave up. She persisted!

PERSONAL RESISTANCES

72

When you hear, 'I wouldn't buy anything from YOU,' you are experiencing a personal resistance.

Don't get me wrong. Gwyneth is a great hairstylist. Its just that, well that she is too direct with people. And it turns a customer off once in a while. Fortunately Gwyneth knows this and rather than have the beauty salon she works in lose that customer, Gwyneth encourages the upset customer to go to another stylist. So while she herself is very opinionated about what's right for her customers, when one of them have a personal resistance against Gwyneth, she can be goal directed, and not ego directed. Her unselfish actions help her salon make the sale anyway.

Personal resistances are in evidence when the customer doesn't buy because of personal factors against the seller. These personal resistances may be conscious, *"I don't like the way my salesman looks, he looks shady,"* or *"I wouldn't buy from her, she's never on time."* When the customer doesn't like the sales person, her personal resistances may also be non-conscious. Non-conscious resistances are occurring when some characteristic of the salesman remind the customer of something negative, maybe even her ex-husband or someone she disliked in her past.

- Re-live times in your life when you didn't buy because you had a personal resistance against the sales person. What are three of the reasons you felt this resistance?
- What are some possible situations that you have or are experiencing where the customer isn't buying because of personal factors?
- What are some possible courses of action you can take?
- Be goal-influenced and don't let your ego take the resistance personally.
- Think big. Make sure your company still gets the sale.
- *"I can understand that you would rather not work with me. It would be unfortunate if you didn't get the product you want because of me. May I recommend our sales consultant Heidi to help you?"*

73 PERSONAL SPACE

Sense how close or far your customer feels comfortable with you in her personal space.

- Sense if your personal space, or comfort zone is narrower or wider than others you meet.
- Be sensitive to the varying personal spaces of your customers.
- Be flexible enough to vary your space after matching the increase or decrease of distance your customer takes.
- Lean forward or outward when your customer does so.
- Remember to match and mirror your customer's distance choice.

"Well, that's our last dinner at that place," she protested

"Why?"

"The waitress sat in our booth to take our order, asked us our names, called us by our first names and acted like she was part of our family. I understand what they are trying to do here, but we have just the family that we want!"

The waitress invaded the family's personal space and lost a big tip. And the restaurant lost some potentially great customers.

In my counseling practice, I always offered my patient three options of seating arrangements, one at a right angle and close, one on the other side of the desk, one on a couch in the background. If the patient hesitated I would then be more directive. Most chose to be separated by the desk, some ventured to the closest seat, and occasionally someone would choose the couch far away. This was my first clue to understand the person's social distance comfort level. I would then watch if the patient pushed the chair further away or moved it closer, and leaned forward or leaned back as we proceeded. Was he relaxed or slouching in his chair?

I would also be interested to see if the person kept a distance and avoided physical contact, shook my hand, or even touched my shoulder while shaking my hand. If the person shook my hand, was he sweating or tense? Was the person interested or curious about me as a person? Did he need to know more about who I am or was he ready to proceed discussing his life? This helped me to understood how long of a rapport phase we needed for him to feel comfortable.

Each customer reveals his levels of comfort through non-verbal information to the sales professional who is sensitive to personal space.

The personal space is the area around the person that the person senses, believes, and feels belongs to her. Any intrusion is a violation and can quickly result in a personal resistance to the sales person.

74

PESSIMISTIC OR OPTIMISTIC EXPLANATORY STYLE?

Pessimists explain setbacks as personal failures and as permanent states,while optimists view setbacks as situation related, and temporary.

Did you know that the difference between the most successful and unsuccessful sales professionals is how they explain to themselves why they missed a sale?

Martin Seligman, psychologist and author of Learned Optimism, studied thousands of life insurance salespersons to discover which qualities make them successful. Seligman discovered that one of the best predictors of success in selling was the salesperson's explanatory style. What is a person's explanatory style? Our explanatory style is how we explain both negative and positive events to ourselves. And Seligman found the pessimists and optimists had two dramatically different explanatory styles in a few ways.

When pessimists face a setback, such as losing a big sale, they explain it in at least two ways that break their sales spirit. The pessimist explanatory style is that "I lost that big sale because (1) 'I'm no good' or 'the customer didn't like me' (taking it personal), (2) and 'I'll never be any good, and no one will ever like me' (making it permanent)."

- You have never failed at anything because you are worthless. The only reason you failed, that time, is because you didn't put the right answers in the right places. Study harder for the next test.
- Explain setbacks to yourself by making them situation related and temporary.
- Recognize the important role that what you tell yourself has in your own motivation.
- Remember, its not what happens to you that affects you; its the way you look at what happens to you that does.

Just think about these self-talk reactions and the stress the pessimistic salesperson creates for himself.

Contrarily, when optimists face the same setback, he uses a quite different explanatory style. The optimistic explanatory style concludes something like "I lost that sale because (1) 'the product or the situation wasn't right' (situation related) or (2) *'it was a bad day' (make it temporary).*" As you can see, the optimist's explanation gives hope and has the salesperson eagerly awaiting the next customer.

75 PHENOMENOLOGIAL SELLING

Your customer operates out of the way that he, not you, looks at life.

- Start by listening to how your customer looks at life.
- Is the customer's view of life, *"I can't afford this!"* even though, in reality, you know this person clearly qualifies?
- Is the customer's phenomenological world , *"I'm not worth it?"*
- Is the customer's phenomenological world, *"I'd feel guilty to buy that?"*
- Understand not only your world, but more importantly the phenomenological world of your customer because it is from their world that they choose to buy or not.
- At the end of the day and you have heard your own sales pitch a dozen times and you are tired of it, realize that to your next customer, your words are fresh and new.
- Avoid making your words robotic and boring. Keep each presentation crisp. If you have a famous historical spot, scene or amusement park near your home that you visited a hundred times before and someone is visiting you from another city who has never been to this great scene, renew your view. See it from fresh eyes.
- Be like Nick Morrow. Start with your customer's world. And every customer has a different view.

So start selling him from his vantage point!

Even though he may like wool suits himself, Nick knows that wool suits irritate my skin. And he wouldn't dream of ever even bringing up the topic with me. Nick Morrow is a master at phenomenological selling. Phenomenological selling is based upon the philosophy of phenomenology, which states *"people operate out of the way they, not I, look at life."* To understand, and to sell someone something, the starting point is the customer's phenomenological world.

Psychiatrist Alfred Adler first observed that each person has his or her *"private logic."* The job of the psychiatrist was to understand the *"private logic"* of the patient. When we do, something interesting happens. All of a sudden, the person's behavior begins to make total sense. Adler argued that, if a person truly believes a snake has bitten him, his actions are consistent with a person who has really been bitten by a snake. This is known as his phenomenological world.

Since the customer operates out of the way he, not the sales person looks at life, phenomenological selling involves understanding, and then selling to the customer's own subjective world (phenomenological world). Everyone has his own *"private logic,"* and the encourager, using phenomenological selling starts with the customer's *"private logic"* of how he is looking at the product.

76

POST PURCHASE COGNITIVE DISSONANCE

Reassure your customer after she makes a major purchase.

Scary, but I have heard variations of this experience more than once. *"There I was at the alter, just said, 'I do' and was sure I just did the wrong thing."* What do these uncertain individuals need now? Some encouragement!

The morning after buying the car, some people are wondering if they made a mistake. Or worse yet, they just signed the papers on their new home and begin thinking of those huge monthly mortgage payments, and all of the other, *"what ifs"* the potential leaky roof, rising real estate taxes, and everything else. This phenomenon of questioning oneself after a major buying decision is known by social psychologists as post purchase cognitive dissonance.

Cognitive dissonance is an unpleasant state whereby a customer is faced with two beliefs that are inconsistent. The person is in a state of temporary imbalance. The customer, in a state of cognitive dissonance, has a psychological need to quickly re-solve this imbalance.

Post purchase cognitive dissonance is occurring shortly after the customer buys a product, especially an expensive one. The customer is experiencing the very natural thoughts of, *"Did I do the right thing?"* or *"Will my sales person still be there for me?" "Is the manufacturer going to support me?"* This is one of the most important moments for our hero, the sales encourager.

- Be obsessive about calling your customer after a big purchase and talk as long as he needs to re-excite him about the product, feel your support and put his post purchase cognitive dissonance to rest.
- Offer very specific facts supporting your reasoning and reassurance.
- Pull out your list that maximizes the benefits and minimizes the risks of buying.
- Remind the customer that you are accessible.
- Get your customer to focus on the membership of owning the product, not on the dues.

77 PROOF

Be loaded with proof of your product's performance.

- Gather data to support the value of your product.
- Compile a list of testimonials from satisfied customers who would be willing to be references.
- Make product comparisons with other similar products.
- Cite specific cases.
- Offer demonstrations whenever possible to support your product.

Bathroom refitters. Every hear of these guys? What do they do? Instead of taking the customer through the cost of removing the old tub or shower, bathroom refitters re-fit their product, on top of your old product.

I needed some bathroom work done but was a little skeptical of this idea. "Why doesn't everyone do this?" I wondered. How could an idea be so simple, yet I missed it for years? As I listened to their story, the magical moment appears. I am handed a list of over 200 names of people with their phone numbers from our city. All 200 plus people have had this same work done and offered to serve as references offering testimonials for the product. And on this list are some names I recognized! If I desired more names, I was informed the saleswoman would gladly provide them. I thought 200 would be adequate. I had the work done, and was very pleased. And, no, I actually never called one single reference. References are powerful proof.

Margaret Holloway, Maryland real estate agent, returns every call within the hour! And she has every bit of information the buyer has requested. She is as quick to give the tough news as she is to give the great news. She is solid and has credibility. Margaret offers proof that your investment is a good one. Proof is powerful.

Proof is the use of reason to move a person from one "*accepted by his current phenomenological world,*" to another truth that will benefit him even more. Some techniques of proof include (1) statistics, (2) special cases, and (3) testimonials from others.

78

QUESTIONS

Always ask questions before telling and selling.

The question a person asks can make a huge difference. The story goes that two priests were wondering if it was ok to smoke while they were praying. They agreed that they would ask the Monsignor. The next evening the two priests started praying and one priest lit up a cigarette.

"What are you doing?" the shocked other priest asked.

"I'm smoking."

"But I asked the Monsignor and he said we couldn't smoke."

"Well," the smoking priest inquired, *"What did you ask him?"*

"I asked him if we it was ok if we smoked while we pray and he said, 'No.'"

"Oh, well I asked him if it was ok if we prayed while we smoked and he said, 'Yes.'"

How we ask a question is vital in sales. Questions uncover information for us.

Questions are a major tool for the encourager because questions direct attention as well as reveal the customer's resistances, objections, sources of discouragement, needs and desired products.

Open-ended questions earn more information than closed-ended questions. Open-ended questions lead to answers that are more than one word.

For example, *"Did you try this product?" "Did you like the product?"* lead to *"yes"* or *"no"* answers. These are closed-ended questions.

"Tell me about your experience with our product!" is an open-ended question and will reveal much more information from the customer.

- Be cautious about asking a question beforehand unless you have reasonable certainty about your customer's answer.
- If in doubt, ask a question. Know the person before selling the product.
- Avoid closed-ended questions (questions that lead to yes or no answers which offer little information).
- Ask questions that are open-ended (open-ended questions are questions that have more than one-word answers, providing more rich information).
- Ask questions to gather information.
- Ask questions using a safe tone and an open body language.
- Ask only one question at a time.
- Ask questions to change the focus of conversation when it is going in a discouraging direction.
- Start to feel comfortable with silences after your question. If so, you will hear very vital information.

79 RECIPROCITY

If someone gives you something, you want to give them something in return.

- How can you use the principle of reciprocity as a salesperson?
- What can you give to your customer just for being there?
- Your time can be a present.
- Have you ever bought something from someone just because she gave you so much time?
- Do you offer coffee, snacks in a special area where people can sit and relax in your business feeling more like they are at your home?
- What do you have to offer that has some value to give to customers such as samples sizes, etc.?
- Reward your customer for showing up!
- Reward your customer for listening!

Robert Cialdini, author of the book Influence, discusses research conducted by P.R.Kunz and M.Woolcot. Cialdini describes a university professor who sent out Christmas cards to random perfect strangers, selected from the local phone book. The results were eye opening. A great majority of those who received his card one year returned a card to him the following year. Even though they didn't know each other! Why did total strangers reciprocate his card?

Cialdini explains why reciprocation works in societies:

"Human societies make sure their members are trained to comply with and believe in it (reciprocation). Each of us is taught to live up to the rule (of reciprocation) and each of us knows the social sanctions and derision applied to anyone who violates it. Because there is a general distaste for those who take and make no effort to give in return, we will often go to great lengths to avoid being considered a moocher, ingrate and freeloader."

Cialdini concludes that humans, in all societies have a need to reciprocate the favors they receive from others. The rule of reciprocation states that *"when someone gives you something, reciprocate by returning to something to them."*

Have you had more than one sample at Panera's Breads? Or tasted the Baskin Robbins new flavor in a cup? If you are like most about half of the people trying the sampled buy that specific product. Almost all buy something. Watch how many people who receive the sample of bourbon chicken at the Mall Food Court choose the chicken rather than the other six choices.

RELATIONSHIP SELLING

80

Include your friendship, help, support and encouragement as part of your product benefits.

Stevie Wonder wrote and sang, *"I just called to save 'I love you.'"* No special event, no big occasion, no birthday.

Building relationships with customers can be some of the most rewarding and profitable parts of a salesperson's work. Vince DeMarco knows about relationship building. And about selling. And he can be patient and build a relationship. Vince is known in Ohio as a great beauty salon sales consultant. One salon, although cordial to Vince, didn't buy anything from the spirited salesman. But Vince kept returning for months, stopping in to say hello, and to keep building the relationship with the potential customer. The owner of that salon decided to build what, at the time was one of the largest salons in the United States, featured on many of the major TV stations and in every relevant magazine. And one Tuesday morning the owner called Vince and asked him to bring in his products.

Vince didn't build a sale. He built a relationship with a customer.

If you shift your goal from selling just today to planting seeds by developing relationship with customers today, something magical happens. Some will return, others will send friends and you can create a momentum of people who enjoy your presence and friendship.

Encouragers learn little things that are important in her life to develop the relationship. Relationship selling has a long-term effectiveness to it.

- Continue to call on that customer who hasn't yet bought from you.
- Bring your customer information, sales tools and let her know that you will be there for her (Accessibility).
- Smile, never leave frustrated, and always learn with a little more information about her business, family, interests, etc.

81 SCARCITY

The less a product is available, the more value the product has.

- When the product is in limited supply, let your customer know, and that will speak for itself.
- *"Don't wait!"*
- *"Limited edition."*
- *"The first 300!"*
- *"These are the few left at the old price."*
- *"THIS IS OUR LAST ONE. AND THEY ARE NOT MAKING ANYMORE!"*

Do you remember the Beanie Babies? How much would you pay for Maple at its highest? Because Maple was better looking or more interesting? No, because Maple was hard to get. I won't tell you what I paid for a Rocky Colavito baseball card!

Robert Cialdini, the world's leading expert on Influence called scarcity, *"the rule of the few."* Cialdini quotes G.K. Chesterton who concluded, *"The way to love anything is to realize that it might be lost."*

Every high school has the unnoticed students who all of a sudden are noticed by one popular person. Soon the person becomes in demand overnight because someone wanted him. The person's appeal level rises. The same person has more value because everyone now wants him or her. And he is scarce because there is only one of him!

In Delaware, one builder offers two properties a month on a lottery. Lines wait to pull numbers for the right to buy. A friend of mine paid his son to arrive a day early to get at least into the lottery line. The properties are beautiful and are gaining thousands of dollars of value each month, plus this promotion guarantees the sale of two pre-construction houses a month. The scarcity principle adds to the value.

When the hurricane is approaching Florida, the price of the dwindling water and gas starts rising. Scarcity communicates a limited number of products and adds value to your product.

SECURITY NEEDS (CUSTOMER)

82

Sell safety to your customer who has security needs.

"Can't get enough safeguards these days," Ed sighed. *"Four dead bolts are twice as good as two as far as I'm concerned."*

OnStar is hot in cars when the driver has a need. Security systems since 9-11 are booming.

Some people are motivated by a desire for heaven; others are driven by a fear of hell. The pleasure seekers and pain avoiders have two dramatically different needs that their products fulfill. The former buys products that will excite their senses or fulfill their dreams. The latter buys products to secure and protect what they have.

The pain avoider is the customer who is driven by security needs. A customer motivated by security has a need for safety from threats, embarrassment, etc. too much pleasure in fact may create guilt or may seem frivolous to the security seeker. The security-oriented customer is more motivated by avoidance of pain than for desire for pleasure. The encourager couples her product in a way that it will fill the customer's security needs.

- How does your product sell security needs?
- Emphasizing that your product is guaranteed, and you will always stand behind it (accessibility) help fulfill a customer who has security needs.
- Use words to connect your client with security needs.
- *"Safe"*
- *"Easy"*
- *"Clear"*
- *"Clean"*
- *"Secure"*
- *"Unbreakable"*
- *"Airtight"*
- *"Secure"*

83 SERVICE RECOVERY

Know your strategy ahead of time, for recovering from service mistakes.

Those of us who were there at the Italian restaurant in Palm Springs that night still talk about it. After bringing our drinks, the perky waitress took our orders. She asked each of us, *"Would you prefer our Italian salad or minestrone soup?"* All five of us chose the salad. A few minutes later the waitress arrives with the salads on one tray and while lowering the tray from her shoulder, all of the salad bowls tilt forward and fall into the laps of two of us... Breaking the silence, the waitress responded, *"Aren't you glad you didn't order the soup?"*

Everyone starts laughing. The manager arrives. The clothes bill will be taken care of as well as the drinks and meals. And next time we were in Palm Springs, all 30 of us went for dinner at our favorite place. This experience could have ended in a dramatically different way.

Nowhere is sales psychology more relevant than in the area of dealing with customer complaints. Consider the following facts:

1. *The average business never hears from 96% of its dissatisfied customers. That means that for every complaint, there are 26 customers with problems.*

2. *Complainers are more likely to do business again with the company that upset them. In fact 95% of complainers will do business with your company again if the problem is resolved quickly.*

3. *The average customer who has a problem tells 9-10 people. 13% tell more than 20 people.*

4. *If the unhappy customer is satisfied with your service recovery, she will tell an average of 5 people. You might turn a service mistake into a positive word of mouth experience with surprisingly great, unexpected, quick service recovery.*

Service recovery is the strategy to handle mistakes and complaints. One service recovery approach is (1) apologize, (2) empathize, (3) solve problem, if possible, (4) give something if not and (5) follow up.

- Be non-defensive, safe, warm, and understanding when approached by a complaining customer.
- Tell your customer at closing time to please call you if she has any problems at all.
- Reading the above statistics, be thankful when a customer complains, rather than walk away and tells 20 of her friends.
- Prepare for your apology. *"I am so sorry that happened to you, Mr....."*
- Prepare for your empathic understanding. *"Its frustrating to go home all excited to use your new..., and it doesn't work!"*
- Prepare for solving the problem. *"We will take care of your problem immediately."*
- Prepare to give something. *"We are out of stock on your brand. However, we don't want you to have one more minute of inconvenience. We can give you a loaner until your arrives, or we will give you an upgrade."*
- Prepare to follow-up. Make that phone call in the next week.

84

SIMILARITY-ATTRACTION PRINCIPLE

Communicate your similarities to your client.

The similarity-attraction principle states: *"The more I perceive you to be like me, the more I like you."*

Dreama was always working. Walking through the new car lot, she would be accumulating information for a curious reason.

Here is her conversation with Dreama's first customer one Spring Saturday:

Dreama: *"Are you from the area?"*

Customer: *"Yeah. Well, Muhlenburg Township!"*

Dreama: *"Did you go to Muhlenburg High School?"*

Customer: *"I'm a Muhl!"*

Dreama: *"Did you know Mr. Dlliplane?"*

Customer: *"He was my advanced placement physics teacher. He was tough, but the best. How do you know Mr. Dilliplane?"*

Dreama: *"He goes to the same health club I go to. I see him almost every day. Ant message?"*

Customer: *"Tell him I went into science because of him. Today, I work at Carpenter Technology in Research & Development."*

Dreama: *"You're kidding. Car Tech. Do you know Len Coleman?"*

You get the point. This sale is in the bag. The skilled salesperson immediately tries to zero in on things she has in common with her customer. Why? Because of the similarity-attraction principle.

The **similarity-attraction principle** states: *"The more I perceive you to be like me, the more I like you."*

- What looks to be small talk can play a big role in selling. Find as many commonalities as you can with your customer. The relationship, and the sale will follow.
- Point out areas of similarities with your customer. Matching and mirroring are effective because of similarity-attraction.
- Listen closely to identify similarities between yourself and your customer.
- Identify product similarities, e.g. Cars, products you sell
- Identify personal preferences, e.g. Colors, sports teams, children's' ages, where you live.
- Share your commonalities with the other person.
- Start using the connecting word, *"we"* or connecting phrases, *"people like us..."*

85 SLEEPER EFFECT

Plant product seeds in your customer's mind that will blossom in the future.

- Plant seeds relating to products that you have available that can be bought at any time needed.
- Plant seeds in your customer's mind that, at some point in the future, when he is experiencing a certain need that he will think of your product. *"When you see dandruff, immediately think....!"*
- Link your product to a certain time or date that the customer will be experiencing.
- Tuesday, 50% off.
- *"On the first snowfall, think.... Tires!"*
- *"Whenever you are feeling...go to....!"*

Albie Boscov is not only amazing and a great businessman. He is a good human being. Growing up in his father Solomon Boscov's popular department store, Albie learned about customer service and sensitivity. Albie today has over 40 stores and has become the single largest privately owned department stores in North America. Today, he spends his energies building downtown Reading, Pennsylvania, and housing the down and out.

Albie's team understood the principles underlying the "Sleeper Effect." The "sleeper effect" occurs when the encourager plants a buying seed that will blossom at some future time in the customer's mind and heart. A few decades ago, Boscov's planted seeds in their customers to think of Boscov's during the whole month of April. Every springtime, hundreds of thousands of Berks County people were motivated by the catch phrase, "Did you Boscov today?" If you showed up at a Boscov store a certain number of days that month and got your Boscov calendar stamped you would earn unbelievable prizes. People began thinking about April as Boscov month, and some even avoided their vacations until May. The seeds were planted, *"When you think April, think Boscov!"*

The sleeper seed can take effect that same day. Burger King's *"Aren't you hungry?"* plants a soon growing seed in our mind preparing us for an early lunch. In fact try a little as experiment I often did. I simply planted seeds for everyone at our office, one by one, by mentioning, *"Couldn't you go for a V&S Cheese Steak Sandwich?"* And then watch everyone in line at the sandwich shop that day. The *"Sleeper Effect"* really is that easy.

SOCIAL COMPARISON

86

Your expressions and feelings about your product are your customer's first clues to your product's value.

Our doctor picks up our tests results and reads it as we intently watch his facial expression. He shakes his head and frowns. We panic. Our heart starts beating heavy. This is a very important test we took. We are thinking, "*Oh my God! How bad is this? What's the worst thing that can happen*?" The doctor continues reading, and starts smiling while nodding his head, and we begin thinking, "*Wheh*!" We experience this whole range of emotion, and the doctor hasn't said a word yet. We were in a state of social comparison.

Social comparison theory states that when people are in doubt about which emotion to experience, they look to others for a clue.

The first time I flew, I didn't realize how turbulence could affect a flight and when the plane started skipping in the sky I was in a state seeking social comparison. Were we in danger? Or were these bumps common? How could I tell? I looked at the facial expression and demeanor of the flight attendant. As she walked calmly up the aisle, and smiled at her customers asking me if I would like a drink, I relaxed. Here we experience social comparison theory at work again.

How do you see social comparison theory fitting in to your sales approach?

- Learn about social comparison by watching people who are selling a product on TV. Watch their demeanor and facial reactions. Observe their enthusiasm. Make notes of their key words.
- Apply what you learned by practicing with your newest product.
- When offering a new product that your customer has never heard of before, your words and demeanor can add value.
- Your enthusiasm about the product adds energy to your customer.
- Your excited facial expression can help your customer to feel and experience your excitement.
- Your calmness can encourage your customer to realize that this is not a big risk.

87 SOCIAL CONTEXT

Control the selling setting because the environment dramatically affects the sale.

- Dyads or two person-selling situations (you and the customer) are easier to manage and to grab attention. Even in a dyad, however, be cognizant if the buyer's decisions will affect others in her social context.
- Identify leaders in the social context who might influence the sale.
- Leaders may or may not be the person buying.
- Identify followers who play no role in the selling process.
- Identify the people who are consulted during the selling process.
- Make sure the decision makers are present during your presentation.
- Ask yourself if the social context is a dictatorship, a democracy, or anarchy.

Most women's dress shops dread children. And yet, women who have children to watch sometimes don't have any other options but to bring the little ones along. So while some shops dread the little ones running through the racks, and forcing mom to leave early, rather than buy, Donna's "*Green Apples,*" in Cocoa Village Florida loves children. Donna gets to know their names, talks to them while mother shops. She remembers the little one's names and inquires about them when they aren't accompanying mom. I've yet to see a mother with a child leave without buying, because Donna understands the social context of buying.

The social context includes all of the human factors present in the selling situation. In the social context, the encourager is aware and observant of each individual who will encourage or discourage the customer from getting the benefits from your product. Do what psychologists call a sociogram. A sociogram is your observation of the social context. Watch the interplay amongst the buying members to identify leaders, followers, cliques, isolates.

SPEED BENEFITS

88

Talk up the speed benefit for people who are impulsive, and want what they want...now!

Very few people want to wait 161 years for their new living room furniture. Imagine if you can guarantee their furniture in 3 weeks! Or what about today or tomorrow! The speed benefit involves customizing and humanizing your service by getting the customer what they faster than the usual amount of time of wait.

- Sense the customer's personality. Impulsive people walk in and want what they want right now. Impulsives (impulsive people) speak fast, move throughout the store fast, buy fast, and unfortunately for the sales person, then sometimes cancel fast. Sell impulsive customers on the speed benefit.
- If you sell products based on significant events, birthdays, weddings, Christenings, bar mitzvahs, sense the timing.
- Give the customer the date of product delivery. Be specific. *"By May 5, you will be driving your new...."*
- If time is the resistance, ask, *"If I could speed up the delivery, would you then be interested?"*
- Whenever relevant and possible, advertise, *"You can leave our store today with your new car, computer or plasma TV."*

89 STATUS MOTIVATION NEEDS (CUSTOMER)

- Customers with status motivation needs will reveal to you in the first few sentences that status is important to them.
- Observe status through a customer's dress, car, speech, vocabulary, bragging, telling you where she usually buys her products, where she lives.
- You know the status areas in your county. Listen for how your customer may or may not emphasize where she is from to indicate if she is motivated by status.
- Where did your customer go to school? Which university?
- Emphasize how your product will enhance a person's standing, give him attention or help him be a part of something bigger than himself.
- Social reinforcements involve recognizing the desired status of your customer.
- Curiously, the person with status motivation needs is an outer-directed buyer. If you respect her status needs, are perceived as believable, she will follow your suggestions.

Sell status and prestige to your customer with status motivation needs.

The name brand person feels nude without the status lifting logo. He will pay extra, a lot extra to show that he is playing in the major leagues of fashion. The extra cost is worth it to him and if you sell upscale products, consider it your responsibility to sell him the product that will fulfill his status needs. He may not be buying a shirt as much as he is buying status, prestige, attention and belonging. Customer satisfaction involves understanding your customer more fully.

STIMULATION NEEDS (CUSTOMER)

90

Sell excitement to the person with stimulation needs.

If your product satisfies stimulation needs, set up your business at the exit ramp of the roller coaster and sell your product to the thrill seekers.

Customers with stimulation needs comes in a variety of forms from thrill seekers to romantics. What people with stimulation needs do have in common is that the salesperson needs to keep them sensually or intellectually engaged during the sale or they are out of there.

A person with stimulation needs is motivated by products and ideas that stimulate the senses. A person with stimulation needs is impulsive, excitable and makes decisions based on sensual stimulation, rather than on logic, reason and what makes sense. An encourager recognizes stimulation needs by a person's stimulating dress, ideas and surroundings.

- Have stimulating music playing in the background, no elevator music for these guys.
- Encourage interactions with your products.
- Couple your product with the person's stimulation needs.
- Actively engage your customer's senses in the selling process.
- Visual senses, *"feast your eyes on this."*
- Auditory senses, *"a beautiful, smooth sound."*
- Tactile senses, *"soft as a lullaby," "this has the strength of a heavy weight champion."*
- Olfactory senses, *"experience this romantic aroma."*
- Gustatory sense, *"beyond gourmet."*
- Some customers need to be stimulated intellectually.
- Talk up the romantic story about the creation of this or that product.

91 SUGGESTIONS

Make that suggestion in your mind.

- *"Might I suggest?"*
- *"If you like the way we did your hair today, we have a way you can keep it looking this great every day at home. Experience the scent of this professional shampoo."*
- *"After you have the awesome and trouble free experience with this product, remember when you come in for a refill you can get twice the size for only 50% more. Fewer trips, save on gas as well as on product."*
- *"Keep in your mind that we have...."*
- *"You really like this style. Always remember that if you have any friends who have similar tastes as you that you can help them experience the same feeling you have today."*
- *"I see you like our... . If you like this, for a few pennies more per ounce, you can have this."*
- How can you use the multi-million dollar idea of suggestion or the *"Supersize"* concept in your work.

It gets me every single time, even though I am prepared to resist it. You know what I mean. Popcorn at the movie theater. The young attendant smiles and says, *"our small popcorn is $4.50, but if you would like a vat of popcorn that we will need to deliver to you in a dump truck to your soft seats during this long movie, that's only $5.00. Only .50 cents more!"* What is anybody going to do?

Suggestions set up expectations. If you are the only person alive still working pumping gas at a gas station and simply suggest to your customer, *"Fill it up?"* you dramatically add to the total sales for the day.

92

SURPRISE

Add value, a good feeling and a great memory by surprising your customer with something she didn't expect.

"*May we please wrap this gift for you?*" the young candy seller asks the elderly man. I have to clear my ears. In today's world there is a place that will actually wrap your gift, without hesitation or hassle. And the sales person actually asks, almost begs to wrap your gift. I hang out at this place when I need some reassurance and can observe how service can be magical. At the mall after you buy your gift from the store, you may get free wrapping if you walk 26 miles to the customer service, and wait in a Disney World sized line, and this heroic little candy seller at Sweet Surprises is going to save you all that work. That is a sweet surprise!

Surprise involves catching a customer's attention by doing something totally unexpected.

Mark Fontaine is the pride of British Columbia for selling professional beauty products. I joined him one day when he explained to me. "*I'm going to surprise my customers today. Watch when the sale begins. When I stop selling and close my order book.*" His customers, who love him, start begging to place an order. Mark, of course, helps them get the products they love. Mark is full of surprises, and he is also many of his customers' very good friend.

- Surprises are fun. Surprise your customers today.
- Go out of character and it will give your regulars energy. Buying energy!
- Remember, no surprises for the person with consistency needs unless your surprise is a better way of doing the predictable.

93 TAG LINES

Turn statements into questions to get your customer involved by tagging on a question at the end of your statement.

- Use tag lines frequently to get the customer involved and into a *"yes"* mood.
- *"Couldn't it?"*
- *"Might it?*
- *"Don't you think?"*
- *"Can't go wrong with this, can you?"*
- *"Awesome, isn't it?"*
- *"Unbelievable, huh?"*

"You know what I mean, don't you?"

"Don't you?" is a tag line. Tag lines are brief questions used by the encourager at the end of a statement that will cue a *"yes,"* set from the customer. *"Looks great under strong lighting, doesn't it?"*

Tag lines get your customer actively involved in the buying process.

TELLING

94

Tell the outer directed person what to do.
*"**You love it. Just buy it now**!"*

Telling is outright recommending to a customer that he should buy your product. The salesperson believes in this product, or in the customer's need for this product so strongly that the sales pro tells the customer to buy it now.

One loyal customer described to me how she totally follows her sales person's recommendation.

"Ginny Guinn tells you exactly what you need to do and which product to buy. She knows what's right for you. She cares and her product delivers every time. Ginny would never mislead a customer. She is like your caring cousin who gives you all of the time you need. She's a real pro. I wouldn't dream of buying from anywhere else."

Encouragers are well aware of the limitations of telling, especially with the inner-directed customer. However telling may be effective with clients who are confused or unsure and the encourager knows the product will benefit them. Telling may also be effective with outer direct person. In general telling is less effective than suggestions, because suggestions will avoid the boomerang, while telling can build up resistances.

- While to be used infrequently, there are times when telling may be effective.
- Void using telling with an inner directed customer.
- *"Grab this now!"*
- The better your relationship and credibility, the more effective telling is.
- Telling may be preceded with, *"As you know, Becky, I don't do this often, but today, I'm going to tell you to grab this property."*

95 TESTIMONIALS

Compile a list of satisfied customers to offer your customer today.

- Make a list of your top 20 satisfied customers.
- Write a brief letter to each person on the testimonial list asking if he or she would be willing to share their experiences with your product and yourself with potential customers. Most will say "*yes*" and be honored.
- If possible offer your testimonials a percentage discount on future purchases.
- Consider using your testimonial givers as your board of advisors to help you serve your customers even better.
- Help your customers to identify with your product, and your success.
- Present your list of testimonials to your new customers who are interested.
- Keep in contact with your testimonial list to get more feedback.
- Update and expand your list of testimonials.

"No thing I can say will sell better than what a previous satisfied customer will say. Its like they speak customereze with each other. Its honest, to the point, addresses the concerns and gets the questions asked that the customer is too polite or tactful to ask the salesman," the award winning Gulf, Ontario Real Estate agent told me.

Testimonials have a credibility that the salesperson, who has something to gain from the sale, may not have. And testimonials can brag about the salesperson. If the salesperson said the same things that the testimonial said about himself, the customer would move a little closer to the door.

UNFREEZING A COMMITMENT

96

Help your customer to buy your idea if it is better than a previous idea he bought.

- Respect previous decisions while pointing out that these choices were made with limited information.
- Minimize your talk about your customer's relationship with the other sales person.
- Maximize your talk on your product's advantages.
- Offer ways for your customer to tell the other salesperson.

Traveling with an insensitive but aggressive insurance salesman years ago, I witnessed the following dialogue:

Customer: *"My future brother in law is an insurance salesman. I told him I will be buying my insurance from him."*

Salesman: *"That's interesting!"*

Customer: *"Why?"*

Salesman: *"Most people don't want their brother in law's nose in their business."*

Customer: *"Hmm, I don't know. What should I tell him?"*

Salesman: *"Tell him that you hope he understands that you feel a little uncomfortable sharing so much of your personal information. Maybe as you get to know each other better, you'd be calling him."*

I couldn't believe it. He won the sale over the salesman marrying his sister. He unfroze a commitment. That was pretty tacky. There are more tasteful ways of unfreezing a customer's commitment to a previous salesperson. What is unfreezing a commitment?

Unfreezing is used when a customer asserts, *"I like your product, but, I'm sorry, I already made a commitment to another product."* The encourager unfreezes the commitment by responding, *"I understand. At the time your thinking was based on the limited information you had available. Today, as you have noticed, you got a bigger picture and found a product that would better serve your needs, didn't you?"* (tag line) *"You have to do what is best for you, don't you?"*

"Believe me, as a sales professional, it happens to all of us that a newer, better, less expensive product comes along and our customer says, 'I'm going to have to go another way.' A sales pro doesn't play games, get upset or try to use guilt. Deep down he understands, and would do the same if he were you."

97 VISUAL BIAS

Sell your visual customer pictures and images.

- Prepare the presentation of your product to appeal to visuals by painting pictures of your product and pictures of its benefits.
- A visual person speaks quickly (as opposed to an auditory person who speaks slowly and deliberately).
- A visual person breathes high in the chest as opposed to an auditory person who breathes from a deeper part of the chest.
- Match the breathing patterns of visuals.
- Speak faster with visual customers.
- Ask the visual questions in ways the visual represents the world

"Is it clear what I'm saying?"

"Do you see it this way?"

"Looks good, doesn't it?"

- When leaving a visual, suggest, *"I'm looking forward to seeing you again."*

Bruce was the college Romeo. He could go on and on in creating a picture in the other freshman boys' minds. One particular picture he painted I still remember. He described this girl he met from Bryn Mawr University. *"Carmella has shiny coal black hair that flows down her confident shoulders. Her facial skin provides the perfect soft background for her pronounced red lips and dark mysterious eyes."* That was just for starters. Bruce painted pictures and the guys in the room with a visual bias were moved.

Customers with a visual bias respond to words that create images, sights and pictures. Visuals use words that reveal how they represent reality to themselves. They see it. When a customer listens to your presentation and responds, *"I see what you mean, it is clear you are with a visual."* Remember people with an auditory bias would respond, *"I hear you."*

Visual people speak faster than auditory people and consequently have a more shallow breathing patter.

WARMTH

98

Be safe, open, warm and understanding.

You never met a warmer salesperson, than Andrea Drewes. Everybody immediately loves her. If you are with her for a even short while you are sure to hear something like, *"Andrea, I can't believe I'm telling you this. I have never told anyone in my life what I am about to tell you!"* Yet, she listens 90% of the time. She communicates her warmth, and customers just open up. No wonder.

Warmth is a psychological and physical close feeling between a customer and encourager. Warmth produces a feeling of non-judgementalism , safety and security.

A warm person is a shelter from the storms of the business world. A warm person has natural verbal and body language skills that communicate genuine interest—a concerned, reassuring caring and safe way of being. A warm person centers on the interests of the other, communicates moment-to-moment involvement through her facial expressions, presents herself with an open body language, and is *"with"* the other person.

Warmth is communicated primarily through such behaviors as caring gestures, posture, tone of voice, touch or facial expressions that tend to bring people closer. The warm sales person has a high level of alertness, and really hears and communicates that she heard not just the words of the other person, but the concerns, and emotions under the person's words. The warm person is in a state of congruence in which her words and her non non-verbal messages are in harmony.

- A warm person smiles, is safe, has open body language, listens to understand rather than judge and responds with empathy and understanding.
- The warmer you are, the more honest your dissatisfied customer will be with you. And, as a result, you will be able to solve the problem and keep your customer.
- Stay focused on the concerns of your customer.
- Be *"with"* your customer.
- Cultivate your open body language as a listener.
- Develop a warm, soothing tone of voice.
- Get into a non-judgmental mindset.

99 WELCOME CRITICISM

When criticized, simply ask yourself, 'How can I use this information to help me become a better person?'

Being goal, rather than being ego influenced is often a difficult journey. Here is another one, maybe even tougher. That is, being a criticism welcomer. But any sales person who can learn this attitude and skill can cut his sales stresses in half! Welcoming criticism skills are the skills to listen to criticism in an open way in order to find opportunities to grow from the observations and assertions of others.

I encourage salespersons to think about the last time a customer criticized them. How did they respond to the critic?

Did they respond out of their ego or out of their goal? Ego responses include blaming the critic, (*"You're not so hot yourself"*), getting angry (*"Who do you think that you are?"* or *"I hate you!"*) and defensive (*"I never did that."*)

Goal responses involve simply asking, *"How can I use the ideas I am hearing to help me become a better person?"*

An ego response leads to emotional pain. A goal response leads to new information that nourishes personal and professional growth, improved relationship, and appreciation of the critic. You do the numbers!

- Listen to the whole story of the critic before responding to any part.
- Convey open body language when being criticized.
- Stay calm and breath deeply.
- Reassure yourself that things will be okay.
- Resist ego responses like "You're crazy," or "You're not so perfect yourself," or "Who do you think you are telling me what to do. I don't tell you."
- Notice all of these ego responses create an emotional problem, and worse yet, give the ego responder no information to grow.
- Make it a goal to learn at least one thing you can use from the critic.
- Welcome the criticism as a source of growth by simply asking yourself, "How can I use what this person is telling me to help me become a better person?"
- Summarize what the critic said to see if you heard her fully.
- Thank the critic!

"YES" MOOD

100

Ask questions to get "yes" answers.

Think about the words and the associated states behind the words, *"Yes"* and *"No."* *"No"* has negative thoughts and feelings associated with it. Watch peoples' body language when they are saying, *"No."* People tend to slightly back off with their head, while putting a little negative look on their face. A little defensiveness and defiance are also associated with *"No."* There is a defensive demeanor, rather than a go-forward spirit to *"No." "No"* holds people back.

Contrarily, when a person is saying *"Yes"* the person's whole mind and body are resurrecting good thoughts and feelings. *"Yes"* is associated with certainty, confidence, growing and forward seeking.

The *"Yes"* mood is occurring when the encourager consciously asks a series of questions that are likely to elicit *"Yes,"* responses from the customer. This creates a *"Yes,"* rather than a *"No,"* mood.

Sales Person: *"You are David?"*

Customer: *"Yes."*

Sales Person: *"And you are looking for a new car?*

Customer: *"Yes"*

Sales Person: *Great"*

"Buying a new car can be exciting, can't it?" (Tag line)

Customer: *"Yes! It sure can."*

- Prepare a few questions that are likely to get "yes" answers from everyone.
- While the person is responding "yes," remember matching and nod your head with a smile.
- When you hear a "no!" quickly get back on track by asking a "yes" getting question.

THE ENCOURAGING SALES PROFESSIONAL EARNS MANY MEANINGFUL PAYCHECKS!

AS A SALESPERSON, you can shape your work into being the best or the worst job possible. It all depends on your view. If your attitude towards selling is "it's just a job", the customer is the enemy and you have to get the customer to buy your product to make money to pay bills, it's a tough job.

If however, you find personal satisfaction in selling, and experience yourself learning and growing from every sales presentation, your work can be very rewarding. You might say that you receive not just a money paycheck, but many other meaningful paychecks, as well. This is especially true when you believe in your product and experience fulfillment in satisfying both your customer's (1) product and (2) personality needs.

The encouraging sales person is self-motivated and driven from within. The encouraging sales person finds internal satisfaction (intrinsic motivation) in her work, as opposed to needing to be pushed, praised, recognized, punished, and threatened by others in the outside world (extrinsic motivation). The intrinsically motivated sales person encourages herself by finding meaning in her sales profession at many levels.

PERSONAL MEANING PAYCHECKS:

1. **PRIDE:** What accomplishment are you most proud of since you started selling?
2. **SELF-ESTEEM:** How has selling changed your beliefs about yourself?
3. **CREATIVITY:** Where have you put your own ideas to use in selling?
4. **PERSONAL GROWTH:** How have you grown since you started selling?
5. **SECURITY:** What security have you earned through the years in selling?
6. **COURAGE:** What was your courageous moment in selling?
7. **CHALLENGES:** What is your biggest challenge today in selling? How can you turn that challenge into a positive?

SALES SKILL DEVELOPMENT MEANING PAYCHECKS:

1. **SKILL REFINEMENT:** What skills have you develop since you started selling?

2. **IMPROVEMENT:** What was the specific idea that you heard or learned that helped you become even better at selling?
3. **PROBLEM SOLVING:** What problems have you helped your company to solve?

PROFESSIONAL MEANING PAYCHECKS:

1. **PROFESSIONAL GROWTH:** How have you grown as a sales professional? What would you have never done in the past that you do as a regular part of your profession today?
2. **RECOGNITION:** What recognition have you received in your work?
3. **ADVANCEMENT:** How have you advanced in your profession?
4. **FUTURE VISION:** Where will you be professionally in 5 years? How much will you be earning?

SOCIAL MEANING PAYCHECKS:

1. **REWARDING RELATIONSHIPS:** What good relationships have you developed in selling?
2. **BELONGING:** With which group do you feel you belong?
3. **ENCOURAGING OTHERS:** Who have you encouraged and helped grow?

SALES TEAM MEANING PAYCHECKS:

1. **PROGRESSING TOGETHER:** What ways is your team progressing?
2. **SHARING A SYNERGY OF IDEAS:** With whom on your sales team do you brainstorm and develop new sales strategies?
3. **TEAM THEMES:** How is your sales team unique, special?
4. **OPEN COMMUNICATIONS:** With whom can you be honest and have great communication?
5. **LEARNING FROM EACH OTHER:** Which of your sales team members taught you the most? Who did you teach?

COMPANY MEANING PAYCHECKS:

1. **FULFILLING COMPANY'S VISION:** How are you helping your company live its vision and values?
2. **FEELING EMPOWERED:** Where has your company trusted you to use your way?
3. **BEING THE DIFFERENCE IN YOUR COMPANY:** Where have you made the difference?

CUSTOMER MEANING PAYCHECKS:

1. **CUSTOMER SENSITIVITY:** Which customer's have you offered your sensitivity to their needs?

2. **EXPERIENCING YOUR CUSTOMER ENJOYING YOUR PRODUCT:** What gives you the most satisfaction about your customer's response to your products?
3. **FIGHTING FOR YOUR CUSTOMER:** When was a time you fought to more effectively service your customer?
4. **ENCOURAGING YOUR CUSTOMER:** Which customers did you believe in and encouraged them to benefit from your products?
5. **CUSTOMIZING YOUR PRODUCT:** Which customers have you done something special for like a speeded up delivery or a customized product?

WORLD MEANING PAYCHECKS:

1. **BUILDING A BETTER WORLD:** What is the single thing that sticks out in your mind as to how your work is building a better world?
2. **TOUCHING LIVES:** How many lives have you touched, directly or indirectly, through your products and services?

INSPIRATIONAL MEANING PAYCHECKS:

1. **SELF-ACTUALIZATION IN SELLING:** What aspect of selling is most fulfilling for you?

2. **FLOWING:** What product do you make the finest presentation often finding yourself, "in the zone" or "flowing?"
3. **PASSION:** What gives you passion and energy in your work?

These are some of the many personal and professional "paychecks" or rewards that the encouraging self-motivated sales professional experiences. Finding deeper meaning in your work can help you build that intrinsic motivation, or your inner drive. And while external rewards are fine, as an intrinsically motivated sales professional, you won't need the constant pats on the back or the recognition plaques. You are your own source of motivation and inner drive. A large part of that motivation is in encouraging your customers to fulfill their needs through your products and services.

As a self-motivated sales consultant, you'll never have to 'go to work' again. Instead go in to learn about and encourage your customer and to create your own personal growth and change the world. And, in that transformational process you change your work life into your lifework!

This book discussed the parallels between selling and encouraging. I encourage you to begin viewing yourself as an encouraging sales professional?

SELLING IS ENCOURAGING

HOW VITAL IS ENCOURAGEMENT in selling? Why wouldn't a customer buy a product that she wants, can afford and both the sales person and customer know it? The encouraging sales professional views some customer's objections as a form of discouragement. (The new car is perfect for your customer; she qualifies for it, but is telling herself, "I'm not worth it." She is discouraged, and may have a self-esteem challenge.) Encouragement is the antidote to discouragement.

The encouraging sales professional experiences the customer as a person who has needs that his product can fill. Some of these needs the customer may have never noticed. Through your encouragement skills, you create an atmosphere to open up the mind of your customer to ideas and products she was not aware existed. (A few years back, I did not even think about buying satellite radio until the sales person went out of his way to introduce it to me. Now it's a part of my life. Thank you, Jack!)

The encouraging sales professional learns everything she can about the psychology of people to understand the customer's needs and motivations. Why? Because, whenever possible, the encourager wants to help fulfill the customer's personality needs through her product. That's called excellence in customer service.

Think about it: Would you rather have your doctor just coldly offer you her product, which is your diagnosis and treatment, or understand your needs, concerns, anxieties and fears while addressing your diagnosis and treatment?

Don't you want you child's schoolteacher to sell the subject matter in a way that is interesting to your child's personality and needs for stimulation?

Don't you demand your Realtor understand that you are turned-off with houses that look like every other house because of your individuation needs?

The encouraging sales person chooses to encourage, rather than to blame the customer. The encouraging sales person uses "phenomenological selling."

Phenomenological selling is recognizing that the customer operates out of the way that she, not the sales person, looks at life. The customer's behavior, from friendly to obnoxious, from passive aggressive to assertive, makes total sense from the way the customer looks at life. This is the customer's phenomenological world. It is the task of the sales person to understand how the customer looks at life. The more the sales person takes this trip into the customer's phenomenological world, the more effective the sales person will be. Stop blaming and start encouraging!

ENCOURAGEMENT SELLING IS NEVER OVER

WHILE THIS BOOK HAS COME TO AN END, selling and encouragement are a continuous process. Long after your retire as a sales professional, I hope that you will continue to use your well developed skills to sell people on making a better world through your social, religious, neighborhood and community groups. And I trust that you will encourage your children and grandchildren to be all that they can.

If anybody can do it, you can. You have the skills to influence, move and shake people up to believe in a better life for themselves to build a better world. You are an encouraging sales professional!

REFERENCES

Brooks, Michael. *Instant Rapport*. New York, NY: Warner Books, 1989.

Cialdini, Robert B. *Influence: Science and Practice, Neeham Heights*. MA.: Allyn & Bacon, 2001.

Dinkmeyer, Don & Lewis Losoncy. *The Skills of Encouragement*. Boca Raton, FL: CRC Press, 1995.

Freedman, J.L. & Fraser, S.VC. (1966) Compliance without pressure: The foot-in-the-door technique, *Journal of Personality and Social Psychology*, 4, 195-203.

Losoncy, Lewis. *Attitude Modification: Motivating Yourself Against All Odds*! Sanford, FL: DC Press, 2005.

Losoncy, Lewis. *Today! Grab It: The 7 Vital Attitude Nutrients to Build the New You*. Boca Raton, FL: St. Lucie Press, 1998.

Losoncy, Lewis. *If It Weren't for You, We Could Get Along: How to Stop Blaming and Start Living*. Sanford, FL: DC Press, 2003.

Losoncy, Lewis. *The Motivating Team Leader*. Sanford, FL: DC Press, 2003.

Losoncy, Lewis. *Turning People On: How To Be an Encouraging Person*. Sanford, FL, DC Press, 2001.

Raven, Bertram H. (DROP: Raven) and Jeffrey Z. Rubin. *Social Psychology: People in Groups*. New York, NY: John Wiley & Sons, 1976

Seligman, Martin. *Learned Optimism*. New York, NY: Alfred Knopf, 1991.

Settle, Robert & Pamela Airlock. *Why People Buy*. New York, NY: John C. Wiley & Sons, 1986.

You can reach Dr. Losoncy...

DC Press / Diogenes Consortium

2445 River Tree Circle

Sanford, FL 32771

407-688-1156

407-688-1135 Fax

Contact@FocusOnEthics.com

Other Books and DVDs by Lewis Losoncy

The Motivating Team Leader

Attitude Modification: Motivating Yourself Against All Odds! (DVD Set)

If It Weren't for You, We Could Get Along! How to Stop Blaming and Start Living

Turning People On: How to Be an Encouraging Person

Retain or Retrain: How to Keep the Good Ones from Leaving

Other Books of Interest from DC Press

366 Surefire Ways to Let Your Employees Know They Count

366 More Surefire Ways to Let Your Employees Know They Count

52 Ways to Live Success... From the Inside Out!

Cut the CRAP... and Resolve Your Problems

E-R: [Employee Retention] — Taking the Lead in Keeping the Best

In Search of Ethics: Conversations with Men and Women of Character

Raising Children One Day at a Time: A Daily Survival Guide for Committed Parents

The Mulling Factor: Get Your Life Back by Taking Control of Your Career

The One Hour Survival Guide for The Downsized: What You Need to Know When You're Let Go

Who Cares: A Loving Guide for My Future Caregivers

Go for the Green! Leadership Secrets from the Golf Course (the Front Nine)

Do I Stay or Do I Go? How to Make a Wise Decision About Your Relationship

Becoming Real: Journey to Authenticity

Unleashing Excellence: The Complete Guide to Ultimate Customer Service

How to Compete in the War for Talent: A Guide to Hiring the Best

Authentic Leadership

Money Came by the House the Other Day: A Guide to Christian Financial Planning and Stories of Stewardship

Cut the CRAP and Make the Sale

Be Happy!